BELIEVE WHAT YOU WILL

PHILIP MASSINGER

NICK HERN BOOKS

LONDON

www.nickhernbooks.co.uk

Other NHB/RSC Titles

John Fletcher
THE ISLAND PRINCESS
THE TAMER TAMED

Ben Jonson
SEJANUS – HIS FALL

Jonson, Marston and Chapman
EASTWARD HO!

John Marston
THE MALCONTENT

Philip Massinger
THE ROMAN ACTOR

Middleton and Rowley
A NEW WAY TO PLEASE YOU

Munday, Shakespeare and Others
SIR THOMAS MORE

William Shakespeare
EDWARD III

The Royal Shakespeare Company

The Royal Shakespeare Company is one of the world's best-known theatre ensembles, and aims to create outstanding theatre relevant to our times. The RSC is at the leading edge of classical theatre, with an international reputation for artistic excellence, accessibility and high-quality live performance.

Gunpowder is a season of explosive political drama to mark both the four-hundredth anniversary of the Gunpowder Plot and the twentieth anniversary of the Swan Theatre. The season of rare Elizabethan and Jacobean plays includes a Shakespeare apocryphal play, a satirical black comedy, and two political thrillers, finishing with a specially commissioned new play.

Building on the success of both the first Jacobean Season in 2002 and the Spanish Golden Age Season in 2004, the RSC is again presenting a body of rarely performed work for a modern audience.

The RSC performs throughout the year at our home in Stratford-upon-Avon and that work is complemented by a presence in other areas of the UK. We play regularly in London and at an annual residency in Newcastle upon Tyne. In addition, our mobile auditorium tour plays in community centres, sports halls and schools in areas throughout the UK with little access to professional theatre.

While the UK is the home of our Company, our audiences are global. We regularly play to theatregoers in other parts of Europe, across the United States, the Americas, Asia and Australasia and we are proud of our relationships with partnering organisations throughout the world.

The RSC is at heart an ensemble Company. Actors, directors, dramatists and theatre practitioners all collaborate in the creation of the RSC's distinctive approach to theatre.

The Royal Shakespeare Company

Patron
Her Majesty The Queen

President
His Royal Highness The Prince of Wales

Deputy President
Sir Geoffrey Cass MA CCMI

Artistic Director
Michael Boyd
Executive Director
Vikki Heywood

Board
Sir Christopher Bland *(Chairman)*
Lady Sainsbury of Turville *(Deputy Chairman)*
Professor Jonathan Bate FBA FRSL
Neil W Benson OBE FCA
Jane Drabble OBE
Janet M Gaymer CBE
Sara Harrity MBE
Laurence Isaacson CBE
Nicholas Lovegrove
Dana G Mead
Andrew Seth
A K Wilson MA

The RSC was established in 1961. It is incorporated
under Royal Charter and is a registered charity, number 212481.

A PARTNERSHIP WITH THE RSC

The RSC relies on the active involvement and the direct charitable support of our audience members for contributions towards our work. Members of our audience also assist by introducing us to companies, foundations and other organisations with which they have an involvement – and help us demonstrate that in return for either philanthropic or sponsorship support, we can deliver benefit to audiences, local communities, school groups and all those who are given enhanced access to our work through private sector support.

RSC PATRONS AND SHAKESPEARE'S CIRCLE

Personal contributions from RSC Patrons provide essential financial support for our artists, educationalists and their students, young writers and audience members that require special access services.

CORPORATE PARTNERSHIPS

The RSC has a global reputation, undertaking more international touring each year than any other UK arts organisation. Our profile is high; our core values of artistic excellence and outstanding performance can be aligned with commercial values and objectives.

Our extensive range of productions, outreach and education programmes help ensure that we identify the best opportunity to deliver your particular business objectives. A prestigious programme of corporate hospitality and membership packages is also available.

For more information, please telephone **01789 272283**

For detailed information about opportunities to support the work of the RSC, visit **www.rsc.org.uk/support**

This production of BELIEVE WHAT YOU WILL was first performed
by the Royal Shakespeare Company in the Swan Theatre, Stratford-upon-Avon,
on 18 May 2005.

The original cast, in order of appearance, was as follows:

PROLOGUE	**Mark Springer**
STOIC	**Nigel Cooke**
ANTIOCHUS	**Peter de Jersey**
CHRYSALUS	**Ian Drysdale**
SYRUS	**Jonjo O'Neill**
GETA	**Peter Bramhill**
BERECINTHIUS	**Barry Stanton**
1st MERCHANT	**Kevin Harvey**
2nd MERCHANT	**Barry Aird**
3rd MERCHANT	**Ewen Cummins**
TITUS FLAMINIUS	**William Houston**
CALISTUS	**Matt Ryan**
DEMETRIUS	**Julian Stolzenberg**
AMILCAR	**Mark Springer**
HANNO	**David Hinton**
ASDRUBAL	**Tim Treloar**
CARTHALO	**Fred Ridgeway**
LENTULUS	**Ian Drysdale**
TAJAH	**Evelyn Duah**
PRUSIAS, KING OF BITHYNIA	**Jonjo O'Neill**
QUEEN OF BITHYNIA	**Evelyn Duah**
PHILOXENUS	**Peter Bramhill**
METELLUS	**Fred Ridgeway**
SEMPRONIUS	**Matt Ryan**
JAILER	**Tim Treloar**
COURTESAN	**Michelle Butterly**
CAPTAIN	**David Hinton**
MARCELLUS	**Nigel Cooke**
CORNELIA	**Teresa Banham**

All other parts played by members of the Company

Directed by	**Josie Rourke**
Designed by	**Stephen Brimson Lewis**
Lighting designed by	**Wayne Dowdeswell**
Music composed by	**Mick Sands**
Sound designed by	**Andy Franks**
Movement by	**Michael Ashcroft**
Fights directed by	**Terry King**
Assistant Director	**Elizabeth Freestone**
Music Director	**Michael Tubbs**
Voice & dialect work by	**Jeannette Nelson**
Casting Director	**John Cannon**
Costume Supervisor	**Poppy Hall**
Production Manager	**Simon Ash**
Company Manager	**Jondon**
Stage Manager	**Zoë Donegan**
Deputy Stage Manager	**Robin Longley**
Assistant Stage Manager	**Juliette Taylor**

The text that follows was prepared by Martin White for the RSC production.
The director, Josie Rourke, has cut some 220 lines from the original,
leaving aside those that are lost or illegible, while Ian McHugh has
provided some 90 lines of new text [contained within square brackets]
where it proved necessary to clarify the action.

CONTENTS

The Gunpowder Season
Gregory Doran

In 2002 the RSC mounted a season of plays by Shakespeare's contemporaries which had rarely if ever been performed since they were written. They ranged from *Edward III*, recently 'canonised' from the apocrypha of Shakespeare, to *Eastward Ho!*, a city comedy by Jonson, Chapman and Marston, to a real discovery, a travel play by Shakespeare's collaborator John Fletcher, *The Island Princess*. Philip Massinger's *The Roman Actor* was set in the reign of the Emperor Domitian, and *The Malcontent* was a sort of revenge comedy by the anarchic John Marston.

The success of the project and the hard work of the ensemble of 28 actors and creative teams was recognised when the season transferred to the Gielgud Theatre, under the auspices of Thelma Holt and Bill Kenwright. When last were Massinger, Marston, and Fletcher on Shaftesbury Avenue? It garnered an Olivier award for the Outstanding Achievement of the Year.

I spent a great deal of time reading the astonishing number of scripts from the period and inevitably had a number of favourites which I was not able to include first time around. Indeed they would fill several more seasons to come, and will, I hope, eventually be reinvestigated by the company. We still have *The Dutch Courtesan* and *Antonio and Mellida* to tackle; along with *Philaster*, *The Sea Voyage*, and *A Trick to Catch the Old One*, *The Staple of the News* and possibly even *Hengist King of Kent*! All treasures in store! However, in considering a follow-up season I have attempted to focus the choice around the impact of the Gunpowder Plot of 1605, 400 years ago this year.

When I was at university in Bristol in the early eighties, an article in *The Observer* attracted my attention. It claimed that a new Shakespeare play had been discovered by a process of computer analysis. That play was known as *The Booke of Sir Thomas More*. I directed the play with a student company, but not as an exercise in opportunistic theatrical excavation, but because, to my amazement, the entire first half of the play concerned a race riot in the City of London. As there were race riots happening just down the road from where I lived in Bristol, in St Pauls, the play seemed particularly relevant. In the play, the riot is eventually quelled by More (in a speech universally credited to Shakespeare, as it happens to be in his own handwriting in the manuscript). The 'strangers' or foreigners to whom the citizens of London take exception were essentially religious asylum seekers, and the current heated debate over asylum makes this aspect of the play once again seem peculiarly resonant.

I am grateful to the late Peter Barnes for alerting me to Middleton and Rowley's *A New Way to Please You*, or *The Old Law*. Peter Barnes, (whose play *Jubilee*, about the Garrick Shakespeare Festival, I directed in the Swan in 2000) was a great enthusiast for the repertoire of this period. He had adapted a version of this brilliant play, for radio, and his endorsement led me to include it, and since his sad death last year, we dedicate this production to him.

The savage premise of *A New Way to Please You* is that all men at the age of eighty and all women at the age of sixty should be eradicated as no longer useful to society. It represents a strain of black comedy which it could be argued developed as a result of the sense of dislocation and a loss of moral moorings in the period following the Gunpowder Plot.

In Massinger's exceptional play *Believe What You Will*, a Middle Eastern leader comes out of hiding and attempts to rally his people, but the might of the Roman superpower hounds him from state to state, threatening any that offer him safe harbour with sanctions and ultimately war. I am grateful to Professor Martin White, our season consultant, for his suggestion that we include this strangely topical play.

Ben Jonson's tragedy *Sejanus* was published in 1605, the very year of the Gunpowder Plot. Jonson uses the Roman Empire as a metaphor for his own age. He describes the virtual police state under which he was forced to operate, with its trumped-up treason trials, and severe attitude to censorship. *Sejanus* is an extraordinary political thriller, and this production marks its first major production in four centuries.

Finally Dominic Cooke, our associate with special responsibility for new writing, commissioned Frank McGuinness to consider the events leading up to 5/11, and the result is *Speaking like Magpies*, which brings our Gunpowder season to a close.

February 2005

INTRODUCTION
Martin White

In the autumn of 1630, Philip Massinger, then the resident play-
wright of the King's Men, the company with which Shakespeare
had been associated, and the most successful theatre company of
the day, wrote a play ostensibly based on events that had taken
place some fifty years earlier. It was, however, considered too
dangerous to license, was not published in its own time, and
survives in a manuscript in Massinger's own handwriting.

Massinger's plays often focus on the collisions and tensions
between the demands of the state and the desires of the
individual, between liberty and control, and the ethical and
social issues that result. They reveal, too, his fascination with
the politics of his day, and inevitably, given the tight state control
of the drama, he at times attracted the attention of the authorities.
His 1619 collaboration with Fletcher, *Sir John van Olden
Barnavelt*, dramatising recent events in the Netherlands, had
been temporarily banned by the Bishop of London, and in 1638
King Charles himself, reading a manuscript copy of Massinger's
The King and the Subject, wrote next to a speech on the issue of a
controversial tax, 'This is too insolent, and to be changed.'

Massinger's new play told of Sebastian, the young and headstrong
King of Portugal, who in 1578 was defeated by the Moors at the
Battle of Al Kasr al Kebir (events dramatised in George Peele's
1589 play, *The Battle of Alcazar*). Despite the Moors' overwhelming
victory (scarcely fifty of Sebastian's army were said to have
survived) and although a body – said to be Sebastian's – was
rendered up by the Moors, many of his countrymen refused
to accept that he was dead, believing he was a 'sleeping king'
who would return (like King Arthur from Avalon) to claim his
throne. This cult – 'Sebastianism' – was to prove a resilient one,
lasting well into the nineteenth century.

Two years after Sebastian's death, Philip II of Spain annexed
Portugal, and various men, claiming to be the lost king, presented

themselves. Two – of peasant origin – were captured in 1584 and 1585. Another, Gabriel Espinosa, a man of some education who found support among members of the Spanish and Austrian courts, was executed in 1594. The fourth was a Calabrian – Marco Tullio – whose story was told in a number of pamphlets, ballads, books and, possibly, a play, that circulated in London in the early 1600s. Tullio was also eventually executed, in 1605.

In telling this story of 'Sebastian's' experiences after his defeat, Massinger appears to have relied mainly on Edward Grimestone's 1612 translation of a French book, de Mayerne Turquet's *General History of Spain*. Grimestone's book (which conflated and expanded other sources) provided Massinger with the outline of 'Sebastian's' wanderings: his time with a hermit, his arrival in Venice (having been robbed by his servants), the arrival of the persecuting Spanish ambassador, his appearance before the Venetian Senate, his escape to Florence and the Spanish pressure on his protectors to surrender him, his imprisonment and humiliation in the streets of Naples and his meeting with the Duke and Duchess of Medina Sidonia.

The play (we don't know its title) was submitted to the Master of the Revels, and censor, Sir Henry Herbert, who noted in his office-book on 11 January 1631 that he 'did refuse to allow of a play of Massinger's, because it did contain dangerous matter, as the deposing of Sebastian, King of Portugal, by Philip the Second, and there being a peace sworn between the kings of England and Spain.'

Massinger set about reworking the play. He appears to have retained largely intact the narrative structure of his earlier version (at one point writing 'Dom Sebastian', later corrected to 'King Antiochus'), but now placed it in a classical setting (as he had successfully employed in *The Roman Actor*, 1626, in which he had alluded to contemporary concerns about the crown's growing autocracy), substituting Rome for Spain, Africa for Europe, Carthage for Venice, Bithynia for Florence, etc. Among the books he turned to in rewriting the play were Sir Walter Ralegh's *The History of the World* and Plutarch's *Life of Titus Flaminius* from which he took the stories of Antiochus, King of Lower Asia, and the Carthaginian general, Hannibal, neither of whom was a 'lost king', but both of whom had opposed, been defeated and hounded by the Romans. Hannibal, for example, was betrayed to the Romans by Prusias, King of Bithynia, and this scene in the play draws very closely on Ralegh. Massinger perhaps at this point gave his play its ambiguous title, *Believe As You List* (the play is performed by the RSC under an adapted title), while a prologue (which is in other handwriting) combined apparent disingenuousness with what looks like a clear pointer to a further, more specific interpretation, suggesting that if his Roman or Asian setting appears to:

> draw too near
> A late and sad example, 'tis confessed
> He's but an English scholar at his best,
> A stranger to cosmography, and may err
> In the countries' names, the shape and character
> Of the persons he presents.

By no longer dramatising the story of 'Sebastian', but rather alluding to it through another story, Massinger had evidently done enough to satisfy Herbert, who licensed the play on 6 May 1631. He noted, however, that it was allowed to be acted only on condition that 'the reformations [i.e., Massinger's alterations] be most strictly observed'. Is it possible that the censor's kinsman, Philip, 4th Earl of Pembroke (who later supported the Parliamentarian side in the Civil War) might, as Lord Chamberlain and, therefore, Sir Henry's immediate superior, have lent some support to the play? Philip was certainly interested in the political application of drama: his copy of the 1625 edition of Chapman's *Byron* plays is extensively annotated, drawing analogies with the situation in the Palatinate (see below).

In 1606, Ben Jonson had observed that 'nothing can be so innocently writ', since 'application' – the tendency to interpret any play as having a further, encoded meaning that needed to be deciphered – had 'grown a trade' with audiences and readers. So what, if any, allusions might Massinger's audience, responding to the prologue's hint, have found in either its original or revised version? What was the 'dangerous matter', beyond a general criticism of Spain? The most likely answer (first argued in 1876 by the historian S.R. Gardiner) is that the play was also conceived of as a transparent analogy for the fate of the protestant ruler, Frederick V, the Elector Palatine (the husband of Charles's sister,

Elizabeth) who had been defeated by the forces of the Catholic League and deposed from his new throne of Bohemia in 1620. Unable to return to their hereditary territory of the Palatinate on the Rhine, partly because of Spanish intervention, the couple (enormously popular in England) were kept in perpetual exile, seeking support from other countries, which King Charles declined to provide.

Herbert makes no specific reference to that possible interpretation, but, significantly, the 'peace' to which he referred in first refusing Massinger's play a licence was the Treaty of Madrid, concluded in November 1630. Many in England saw the protestant and Palatine causes as synonymous, and the Treaty, perceived to be based on promises by Spain rather than real concessions, was widely considered to be a betrayal of both. Indeed, it was later described in The Grand Remonstrance of 1641 (John Pym's savagely critical assessment of Charles's reign) as the means 'Whereby the Palatine's cause was deserted'.

Of course, for a modern audience, while these speculations on the play's possible impact on its original audiences are of historical interest, they do not, in themselves, provide reason to revive the play. Its strength must lie in how Massinger's portrayal of a 'world of politic windings' also speaks directly to us now. Crucially, Massinger makes it clear that no one, friend *or* enemy, doubts the veracity of Antiochus's claim. In so doing, he stresses that decisions to support or abandon Antiochus are pragmatic not principled, and depicts a world where the values of honour, truth and justice can be 'frighted' from people by 'power', and where personal freedoms and beliefs are all vulnerable to the 'necessity of state'. It is a world in which, as a mighty military power enforces its political will, men and women see themselves as 'buildings of faith and virtue' under attack, seeking to create defences for their safety, but buildings inevitably besieged, eventually destroyed and left in ruins. As Antiochus tells Marcellus, at the play's bleak and uncompromising conclusion, in which, characteristically, Massinger leaves his contradictions unresolved: 'You must not see / The sun, if, in the policy of state, / It is forbidden.'

The Text

Massinger's play survives in a manuscript, one of only eighteen manuscript playbooks (i.e., prepared for production in the playhouse) known to be in existence (*Sir Thomas More* and Massinger's own *Barnavelt* and *The Parliament of Love* among them). The manuscript is of particular interest, however, as it is in Massinger's own handwriting. The production details it contains, more extensive than in the majority of the other playbooks, are the work of Edward Knight, the King's Men's book-keeper. The equivalent of a modern stage manager, Knight marked up the play for performance, possibly wrote out the Prologue and Epilogue, and prepared a short list of personal properties required by the actors. His annotations also make it possible to identify the original cast, who included the company's leading actors Joseph Taylor as Antiochus and John Lowin as Flaminius. The manuscript also reveals the intriguing fact that two actors shared the role of Calistus and that three played the part of Demetrius. The final page of the manuscript bears Herbert's licence and his signature. The play was never printed in its own time; the first edition came in 1849.

The date of Massinger's first version and some of Knight's markings suggest that the play was primarily intended for the company's indoor playhouse at Blackfriars rather than the outdoor Globe. Apart from a production at Bristol University in 2001, I know of no performance of the play since any that might have been given before 1642.

Henry Herbert occasionally complained of the untidy or illegible state of plays submitted to him, but Massinger's is a very clear copy (perhaps because he was to a large extent copying from the original, making his changes as he went). However, as a result of wear and tear the manuscript is damaged (it was evidently rescued from 'a vast mass of rubbish' in the 1840s) and parts of the play are missing or indecipherable. One page has been torn out almost completely, leaving only a narrow strip and a few half-words, while other damage has caused text to be lost at the top and bottom of a number of pages. For this production, therefore, and very much in the spirit of authorial collaboration, another writer, Ian McHugh, has provided some 90 lines of new text, where it proved necessary to clarify the action. This new text is contained within square brackets.

The text printed here is that performed by the RSC and based on a modernised text specially prepared for the production by Martin White. The director, Josie Rourke, has cut some 220 lines from the original, leaving aside those that are lost or illegible. The manuscript is held in the British Library (Egerton 2828) and a complete, old spelling text can be found in Volume III of *The Plays and Poems of Philip Massinger*, edited by Philip Edwards and Colin Gibson, Oxford University Press, 1976.

Martin White is Professor of Theatre at the University of Bristol and the Consultant on the RSC Gunpowder Season. His publications include Middleton and Tourneur *(1992) and* Renaissance Drama in Action *(1998). He has recently completed work on an edition of Massinger's* The Roman Actor *for the Revels series.*

BELIEVE WHAT YOU WILL

originally
Believe As You List

CHARACTERS

Prologue
Stoic
Antiochus
Chrysalus
Syrus
Geta
Berecinthius
Merchants
Titus Flaminius
Calistus
Demetrius
Amilcar
Hanno
Asdrubal
Carthalo
Officers
Lentulus
Tajah
King Prusias
Prusias's Queen
Philoxenus
Metellus
Sempronius
Jailer
Courtesan
Marcellus
Cornelia
Captain
Soldiers
Servants
Stoics

PROLOGUE

So far our author is from arrogance,
That he craves pardon for his ignorance
In story. If you find our Roman Empire here,
Or hapless Asian continent, draw too near
A late and sad example, 'tis confessed
He's but an English scholar at his best,
A stranger to cosmography, and may err
In the countries' names, the shape and character
Of the persons he presents. Yet he is bold
In me to promise, be it new or old,
The tale is worth the hearing; and may move
Compassion, perhaps deserve your love.
You sit his judges, and, like judges, be
From favour to his cause, or malice, free;
Then, if he labours true or squanders skill,
As the title speaks, Believe What You Will!

ACT ONE

SCENE ONE

Enter Antiochus, the Stoic in a philosopher's habit,
Chrysalus, Syrus and Geta (servants to Antiochus).

Stoic   You are now in sight of Carthage, that great city
Which in her empire's vastness rivals Rome
At her proud height. Two hours will bring you thither.
Make use of what you have learned in your long
                               travails,
And from the golden principles read to you
In th'Athenian Academy. Stand resolved
For either fortune. You must now forget
The contemplations of a private man
And put in action that which may comply
With the majesty of a monarch.

Antiochus   How that title –
That glorious attribute of majesty,
That troublesome, though most triumphant robe
Designed me in my birth, which I have worn
With terror and astonishment to others –
Affrights me now. O memory, memory
Of what I was once, when the Eastern world
With wonder in my May of youth looked on me.
Ambassadors of the most potent kings –
With noble emulation contending
To court my friendship – their fair daughters offered
As pledges to assure it, with all pomp
And circumstance of glory. Rome herself,
And Carthage, emulous whose side I should
Confirm in my protection. O remembrance,
With what ingenious cruelty and tortures,
Out of a due consideration of
My present low and desperate condition
Dost thou afflict me now.

Stoic
                                  You must oppose
(For so the stoic discipline commands you)
That wisdom, with your patience fortified,
Which holds dominion over fate, against
The torrent of your passion.

Antiochus
                                         I should,
I do confess I should – if I could drink up
That river of forgetfulness poets dream of.
But still in dreadful forms – philosophy wanting
Power to remove 'em – all those innocent spirits,
Borrowing again their bodies gashed with wounds,
Which strewed Achaia's bloody plains, and made
Rivulets of gore, appear to me, exacting
A strict account of my ambitious folly
For the exposing of twelve thousand souls
(Who fell that fatal day) to certain ruin.
Neither the counsel of the Persian king
Prevailing with me, nor the grave advice
Of my Roman enemy, Marcus Scaurus, hind'ring
My desperate enterprise, too late repented.
Methinks I now look on my butchered army –

Stoic   This is mere melancholy.

Antiochus
                                  O 'tis more, sir.
Here, there, and everywhere they do pursue me.
The Genius of my country, made a slave,
Like a weeping mother seems to kneel before me,
Wringing her manacled hands; the hopeful youth
And bravery of my kingdom in their pale
And ghastly looks lamenting that they were
Too soon by my means forced from their sweet being.
[I see them – spotless maids bow down before soldiers'
Lust and lift unyielding eyes to ask protection
That I cannot offer. I would unwind fate,
Yet I cannot rescind; I see them] sold
Under the spear. Consider then if it can be
In the constancy of a stoic to endure
What now I suffer.

Stoic
                                ·   Two and twenty years

Travelling o'er the world you have paid the forfeit
Of this engagement, and shed a sea of tears
In your sorrow for it. And now, being called from
The rigour of a strict philosopher's life
By the cries of your poor country, you are bound
With an obedient cheerfulness to follow
The path that you are entered in, which will
Guide you out of a wilderness of horror
To the flourishing plains of safety, the just gods
Smoothing the way before you.

Antiochus   Though I grant
That all impossibilities are easy
To their omnipotence, give me leave to fear
The more than doubtful issue. Can it fall
In the compass of my hopes the lordly Romans,
So long possessed of Asia, will e'er part with
A prey so precious and dearly purchased?
A tigress circled with her famished whelps
Will sooner yield a lamb snatched from the flock
To the dumb oratory of the ewe
Than Rome restore one foot of earth that may
Diminish her vast empire.

Stoic   In her will
This may be granted. But you have a title
So strong and clear, that there's no colour left
To varnish Rome's pretences. Add this, sir:
The Asian princes, warned by your example,
And yet unconquered, never will consent
That such a foul example of injustice
Shall to the scandal of the present age
Hereafter be recorded. They in this
Are equally engaged with you, and must,
Though not in love to justice, for their safety,
In policy assist, guard, and protect you.
And you may rest assured, it cannot pass
That this great Carthage, grown already jealous
Of Rome's encroaching empire, will cry aim
To such an usurpation, which must
Take from their own security. Besides,

> Your mother was a Roman. For her sake,
> And the families from which she is derived,
> You must find favour.

Antiochus   For her sake, alas, sir,
> Ambition knows no kindred. 'Right and lawful'
> Was never yet found as a marginal note
> In the black book of profit. I am sunk
> Too low to be buoyed up.

[*Stoic*   You are in sight of Carthage;
> Do not forget your purpose, nor the laborious
> Devotions of your learning. Avow thy misdeeds
> And own thy mistakes – every circumstance leads
> To truth. Yield to this, you proceed unhindered.

Further Stoics enter with water. The Stoic begins the ceremony.

Antiochus   I will proceed with open hands, and stand resolved
> For either fortune.

Syrus kills the Stoic.

Geta takes Antiochus's possessions and exchanges the water for blood.

> Carthage will hear me;
> The Senate will give me wise counsel.
> They will know the bloody sorrow of a wretched
> And forsaken king.

Chrysalus anoints Antiochus's head with blood.

> I am cleansed.

Chrysalus holds a knife to Antiochus's throat.

Chrysalus   Your recklessness has let this blood, Antiochus,
> The forfeit of your twelve thousand men, not
>   forgotten.
> It rains upon you, does not fall from your ill skin;
> It sticks. A fool would return your kingdom to you.
> These twenty-two years, your brutal folly
> Has been the death-weight on my service to you.
> I fought for your land, I followed sanctimonious
> Command; twelve thousand slain, yet we are all dead,

Abetting your vain and bootless cause. You have

                                              made us

Dead. The world is no longer yours, Antiochus.
You are no king. Rome will crush you. As we reclaim
Our living breath, your kingdom is oblivion.

Releases Antiochus.

Chrysalus, Syrus and Geta flee.

Antiochus   This blood, it sticks. This corruption of fate
Is not my decree, this is wickedness.
Thou hast enacted a despicable trespass,
A most abominable desecration.
I do not cease to remember the valour
Of my men, of every being lost to me,
But you forget your duty to the king.
There is nothing vain in truth – I elected
My path in good faith, as I am truth's servant,
I followed into battle with infallible
Belief.

He regards the Stoic.

I did not wish this. How does a man
Not surrender to wrath when he looks on
The spilt blood of his friend; how does he not contest
With contrition, the balance of his shame?
What service hast thy principles now, old man,
What profit thy discipline? This abject deed
I will not own. My friend, thou hast led me
In sight of Carthage;] can I, in this weed
And without gold, nourish hope
Of a recovery? Forlorn majesty,
Wanting the outward gloss and ceremony
To give it lustre, meets no more respect
Than knowledge with the ignorant. Ha! What is
Contained in this waste paper? (*Reads*) 'Tis endorsed
'To the no king Antiochus'; and subscribed
'No more thy servant but superior, Chrysalus'.
What am I fallen to? There is something writ more.
Why this small piece of silver? What I read may
Reveal the mystery: 'Forget thou wert ever

Called King Antiochus. With this charity
I enter thee a beggar.' Too-tough heart,
Will nothing break thee? O that now I stood
On some high pyramid from whence I might
Be seen by the whole world, and with a voice
Louder than thunder pierce the ears of proud
And secure greatness with the true relation
Of my remarkable story, that my fall
Might not be fruitless, but still live the great
Example of man's frailty. I that was
Born and bred up a king, whose frown or smile
Spake death or life, my will a law, my person
Environed with an army, now exposed
To the contempt and scorn of my own slave
Who, in his pride, as a god compared with me,
Bids me become a beggar. But complaints
Are weak and womanish. I will, like a palm tree,
Grow under my huge weight. Nor shall the fear
Of death or torture that dejection bring
To make me live, or die, less than a king.

Exit.

SCENE TWO

Enter Berecinthius, a flamen, with three Asian Merchants.

1 Merchant   We are grown so contemptible he disdains
              To give us hearing.

2 Merchant   Keeps us off at such distance,
              And with his Roman gravity declines
              Our suit for conference.

3 Merchant   A statesman?
              The devil, I think, who only knows him truly,
              Can give his character. When he is to determine
              A point of justice, his words fall in measure
              Like plummets of a clock, observing time
              And just proportion.

1 Merchant   But when he is
          To speak in any cause concerns himself
          Or Rome's republic, like a gushing torrent
          Not to be stopped in its full course, his reasons,
          Delivered like a second Mercury,
          Break in and bear down whatsoever is
          Opposed against 'em.

2 Merchant   When he smiles, let such
          Beware as have to do with him, for then,
          Sans doubt, he's bent to mischief.

Berecinthius   As I am
          Cybele's flamen, whose most sacred image,
          Drawn thus in pomp, I wear upon my breast,
          I am privileged. Nor is it in his power
          To do me wrong. And he shall find I can
          Chant, and aloud, too, when I am not at
          Her altar kneeling. Mother of the gods, what is he
          At his best but a patrician of Rome,
          His name Titus Flaminius. And speak mine –
          Berecinthius, Archflamen to Cybele –
          It makes as great a sound.

1 Merchant   True. But his place, sir,
          And the power it carries in it, as Rome's legate,
          Gives him pre-eminence o'er you.

Berecinthius   Not an atom.
          When moral honesty and *jus gentium* fail
          To lend relief to such as are oppressed,
          Religion must use her strength. I am perfect
          In these notes you gave me. Do they contain at full
          Your grievances and losses?

1 Merchant   Would they were
          As well redressed as they are punctually
          Delivered to you.

Berecinthius   Say no more. They shall,
          And to the purpose.

2 Merchant   Here he comes.

Enter Titus Flaminius, Calistus and Demetrius

Berecinthius	Have at him.

Flaminius   (*Indicating the Merchants*)
Blow away these troublesome and importunate drones.
I have embryos of greater consequence
In my imaginations to which
I must give life and form, not now vouchsafing
To hear their idle buzzes.

1 Merchant   Note you that.

Berecinthius Yes, I do note it, but the flamen is not
So light to be removed by a groom's breath.
I must, and will, speak, and I thus confront him.

Flaminius   But that the image of the goddess which
Thou wear'st upon thy breast protects thy rudeness,
It had forfeited thy life. Dost thou not tremble
When an incensèd Roman frowns?

Berecinthius   I see
No Gorgon in your face.

Flaminius   Must I speak in thunder
Before thou wilt be awed?

Berecinthius   I rather look
For reverence from thee, if thou respect'st
The goddess' power, and in her name I charge thee
To give me hearing.   (*Indicating the emblem on his chest.*)
                    If these lions roar
For thy contempt of her, expect a vengeance
Suitable to thy pride.

Flaminius   Thou shalt o'ercome.
There's no contending with thee.

3 Merchant   Hitherto
The flamen hath the better.

1 Merchant   But I fear
He will not keep it.

Berecinthius   Know you these men's faces?

Flaminius   Yes, yes. Poor Asiatics.

Berecinthius   Poor they are made so
By your Roman tyranny and oppression.

Flaminius   Take heed:
If arrogantly you presume to tax
The Roman government, your goddess cannot
Give privilege to it, and you'll find – and feel –
'Tis little less than treason, flamen.

Berecinthius   Truth
In your pride is so interpreted. These poor men,
These Asiatic merchants, whom you look upon
With such contempt and scorn, are they to whom
Rome owes her bravery. Their industrious search
To the farthest Indies, with danger to themselves,
Brings home security to you, to you unthankful.
Your magazines are from their sweat supplied;
The legions with which you fright the world
Are from their labour paid; the Tyrian fish,
Whose blood dyes your proud purple, in the colour
Distinguishing the senator's guarded robe
From a plebeian habit, their nets catch;
The diamond hewed from the rock, the pearl
Dived for into the bottom of the sea,
The sapphire, ruby, hyacinth, amber, coral,
And all rich ornaments of your Latin dames
Are Asian spoils. They are indeed the nerves
And sinews of your war, and without them
What could you do? – Your handkerchief?

Flaminius   Wipe your face,
You are in a sweat. The weather's hot; take heed
Of melting your fat kidneys.

Berecinthius   There's no heat
Can thaw thy frozen conscience.

Flaminius   To it again now; I am not moved.

Berecinthius   I see it. If you had
The feeling of a man, you would not suffer
These men, who have deserved so well, to sink

Under the burden of their wrongs. If they
Are subjects, why enjoy they not the rights
And privilege of subjects? What defence
Can you allege for your connivance to
The Carthaginian galleys who forced from 'em
The prize they took, belonging not to them
Nor their confederates?

Flaminius   With reverence
To your so sacred goddess, I must tell you
You are grown presumptuous, and in your demands
A rash and saucy flamen. Meddle with
Your juggling mysteries, and keep in awe
Your gelded ministers. Shall I yield account
Of what I do to you?

1 Merchant   He smiles in scorn.

2 Merchant Nay then, I know what follows.

3 Merchant   In his looks
A tempest rises.

Flaminius   How dare you complain?
Or in a look repine? Our government
Hath been too easy, and the yoke which Rome
In her accustomed lenity imposed
Upon your stubborn necks begets contempt.
Hath our familiar commerce and trading,
Almost as with our equals, taught you to
Dispute our actions? Have you quite forgot
What we are and you ought to be? Shall vassals
Capitulate with their lords?

2 Merchant   Ay, now he speaks
In his own dialect.

Flaminius   'Tis too frequent, wretches,
To have the vanquished hate the conqueror,
And from us needs no answer. Do not I know
How odious the lordly Roman is
To the despisèd Asian, and that
To gain your liberty you would pull down
The altars of your gods, and like the giants
Raise a new war 'gainst Heaven?

1 Merchant   Terrible.

Flaminius   Did you not give assurance of this when
             Giddy Antiochus died? And rather than
             Accept us guardians of your orphan kingdom,
             When the victorious Scaurus with his sword
             Pleaded the Roman title, with one vote
             You did exclaim against us as the men
             That sought to lay an unjust grip upon
             Your territories, ne'er rememb'ring that
             In the brass-leaved book of fate it was set down
             The earth should know no sovereign but Rome.
             Yet you repined, and rather chose to pay
             Homage and fealty to the Parthian,
             Th'Egytian Ptolemy, or indeed any,
             Than bow unto the Roman.

Berecinthius   And perhaps
             Our government in them had been more gentle,
             Since yours is insupportable.

Flaminius   If thou wer't not
             In a free state, the tongue that belcheth forth
             These blasphemies should be seared.
             (*To Merchants*)   For you, presume not
             To trouble me hereafter. If you do,
             You shall, with horror to your proudest hopes,
             Feel really that we have iron hammers
             To pulverise rebellion, and that
             We dare use you as slaves.
             (*To Berecinthius*)   Be you, too, warned, sir,
             Since this is my last caution: I have seen
             A murmurer like yourself, for his attempting
             To raise sedition in Rome's provinces,
             Hanged up in such a habit.

                        Exeunt Flaminius, Calistus and Demetrius.

Berecinthius   I have took
             Poison in at my ears, and I shall burst
             If it come not up in my reply.

1 Merchant   He's gone, sir.

Berecinthius   He durst not stay me. If he had, had found
          I would not swallow my spittle.

2 Merchant   As we must
          Our wrongs and our disgraces.

3 Merchant   O the wretched
          Condition that we live in, made the anvil
          On which Rome's tyrannies are shaped and fashioned.

1 Merchant   But our calamities, there is nothing left us
          Which we can call our own.

2nd Merchant   Our wives and daughters
          Lie open to their lusts, and such as should be
          Our judges dare not right us.

3 Merchant   O Antiochus!
          Thrice happy were the men whom fate appointed
          To fall with thee in Achaia.

2 Merchant   They have set
          A period to their miseries.

Berecinthius   If religion
          Be not but a mere word only, and the gods
          Are just, we shall find a delivery
          When least expected.

1 Merchant   'Tis beyond all hope, sir.

                    Enter Antiochus.

Berecinthius   Ha! Who is this?

Antiochus   Your charity to a poor man,
          As you are Asians.

2 Merchant   Pray you observe him.

3 Merchant   I am amazed!

1 Merchant   I, thunderstruck.

Berecinthius   What are you?

Antiochus   The King Antiochus.

1 Merchant   Or some deity
          That hath assumed his shape.

Berecinthius   He only differs
In the lineament of his face, and age.

Antiochus   Consider
What two and twenty years of misery
Can work upon a wretch.

1 Merchant   His own voice.

2 Merchant His very countenance. His forehead. Eyes.

3 Merchant His nose. His very lip.

Berecinthius   His stature. Speech.

2 Merchant   The moles upon
His face and hands.

3 Merchant   The scars caused by his hurts
On his right brow and head.

Berecinthius   The hollowness
Of his under jaw occasioned by the loss
Of a tooth pulled out by his surgeon.

1 Merchant   To confirm us,
Tell us your surgeon's name when he served you.

Antiochus You all knew him
As I do you – Demetrius Castor.

2 Merchant Strange.

3 Merchant   But most infallibly true.

Berecinthius   So many marks
Confirming us we sin in our distrust.
A sacrifice for his safety.

1 Merchant   May Rome sink.

2 Merchant And Asia once more flourish.

3 Merchant   You the means, sir.

Antiochus Silence your shouts. I will give stronger proofs
Than these exterior marks when I appear
Before the Carthaginian senators,
With whom I have held more intelligence

And private counsels than with all the kings
Of Asia or Africa. I'll amaze them
With the wonder of my story.

Berecinthius   Yet until
Your majesty be furnished like yourself,
To a neighbour village.

Antiochus   Where you please. The omen
Of this encounter promises a good issue.
And, our gods pleased, oppressèd Asia,
When aid is least expected, may shake off
Th'insulting Roman bondage, and in me
Gain and enjoy her pristine liberty.

Exeunt.

ACT TWO

SCENE ONE

Enter Flaminius and Calistus.

Flaminius   A man that styles himself Antiochus, say you?

Calistus   Not aloud styled so, but as such received
And honoured by the Asians.

Flaminius   Two impostors,
For their pretension to that fatal name,
Already have paid dear, nor shall this third
Escape unpunished.

Calistus   'Twill exact your wisdom,
With an Herculean army (the cause requires it),
To strangle this new monster in the birth.
For on my life he hath delivered to
The credulous multitude such reasons why
They should believe he is the true Antiochus,
That, with their gratulations for his safety
And wishes for his restitution, many
Offer the hazard of their lives and fortunes
To do him service.

Flaminius   Poor seducèd fools.
With one puff, thus I will disperse and scatter
This heap of dust. Here, take my ring: by this
Entreat my friend Amilcar to procure
A mandate from the Carthaginian Senate
For the apprehension of this impostor,
And with all possible speed.

Exit Calistus.

               How e'er I know
The rumour of Antiochus' death uncertain,
It much imports the safety of great Rome
To have it so believed.

Enter Demetrius.

Demetrius   There wait without
Three fellows I ne'er saw before, who much
Importune their access. They swear they bring
Business along with 'em that deserves your ear,
It being for the safety of the republic
And quiet of the provinces. They are full
Of gold; I have felt their bounty.

Flaminius   Such are welcome.
Give them admittance.

                               Exit Demetrius.

                     In this various play
Of state and policy, there's no property
But may be useful.

       Enter Demetrius, Chrysalus, Geta, Syrus.

                    Now, friends, what designs
Carry you to me?

Geta   My most honoured lord –

Syrus   May it please your mightiness –

Flaminius   Let one speak for all.
I cannot brook this discord.

Chrysalus   As our duties
Command us, noble Roman, having discovered
A dreadful danger, with the nimble wings
Of speed approaching to the state of Rome,
We hold it fit you should have the first notice,
That you may have the honour to prevent it.

Flaminius   I thank you. But instruct me – what form wears
The danger that you speak of?

Chrysalus   It appears
In the shape of King Antiochus.

Flaminius   How! Is he
Rose from the dead?

Chrysalus	Alas, he never died, sir.

He at this instant lives. The more the pity
He should survive, to the disturbance of
Rome's close and politic counsels, in the getting
Possession of his kingdom which he would
Recover (simple as he is) the plain
And downright way of justice.

Flaminius   Very likely.
But how are you assured this is Antiochus,
And not a counterfeit? Answer that.

Chrysalus   I served him
In the Achaian war, where, his army routed,
And the warlike Romans hot in their execution,
To shun their fury he and his minions were –
Having cast off their glorious armour – forced
To hide themselves as dead, with fear and horror,
Among the slaughtered carcasses. I lay by them,
And rose with them at midnight. Then retiring
Unto their ships we sailed to Corinth, thence
To India, where he spent many years
With their gymnosophists. There I waited on him,
And came thence with him. But, at length, tired out
With an unrewarded service, and affrighted
In my imagination with the dangers,
Or rather certain ruins, in pursuing
His more than desperate fortunes, we forsook him.

Flaminius A wise and politic fellow. Give me thy hand.
Thou art sure of this?

Chrysalus   As of my life.

Flaminius   And this is
Known only to you three?

Chrysalus   There's no man lives else
To witness it.

Flaminius   The better. But inform me,
And, as you would oblige me to you, truly –
Where did you leave him?

Syrus   For the payment of
               Our long and tedious travel we made bold
               To rifle him.

Flaminius   Good.

Geta   And so disabling him
               Of means to claim his right, we hope despair
               Hath made him hang himself.

Flaminius   It had been safer
               If you had done it for him. But, as 'tis,
               You are honest men. You have revealed this secret
               To no man but myself?

Chrysalus   Nor ever will.

Flaminius   (Aside) I will take order that you never shall. –
               And since you have been true unto the state
               I'll keep you so. I am even now considering
               How to advance you.

Chrysalus   What a pleasant smile
               His honour throws upon us.

Geta   We are made.

Flaminius   My house shall be your sanctuary.

Syrus   There's a favour.

Flaminius   And that our entertainment come not short
               Of your deservings, I commit you to
               My secretary's care.
               (To Demetrius)   See that they want not
               Among their other delicates.

Chrysalus   Mark that.

Flaminius   (Aside to Demetrius) A sublimated pill of mercury
               For sugar to their wine.

Demetrius   (Aside)   I understand you.

Flaminius   Attend these honest men as if they were
              Made Roman citizens. And be sure at night
              I may see 'em well lodged.
              (*Aside to Demetrius*)   Dead in the vault I mean.
              Their gold is thy reward.

Demetrius   (*Aside*)   Believe it done, sir.

Flaminius   And when 'tis known how I have recompensed
              (Though you were treacherous to your own king)
              The service done to Rome, I hope that others
              Will follow your example. Enter, friends;
              I'll so provide that when you next come forth
              You shall not fear who sees you.

Chrysalus   Was there ever
              So sweet a tempered Roman?

Flaminius   You shall find it.

                                      Exeunt all but Flaminius.

              – Ha! What's the matter? Do I feel a sting here,
              For what is done to these poor snakes? My reason
              Will easily remove it. That assures me
              That, as I am a Roman, to preserve
              And propagate her empire, though they were
              My father's sons, they must not live to witness
              Antiochus is in being. The relation
              The villain made in every circumstance
              Appeared so like to truth that I began
              To feel an inclination to believe
              What I must have no faith in. By my birth
              I am bound to serve thee, Rome, and what I do
              Necessity of state compels me to.

                                                    Exit.

SCENE TWO

Enter Amilcar, Hanno, Asdrubal, Carthalo, with Officers.

Amilcar   To steer a middle course 'twixt these extremes
             Exacts our serious care.

Hanno   I know not which way
             I should incline.

Amilcar   The reasons this man urges
             To prove himself Antiochus are so pregnant,
             As not to show him our compassion were
             A kind of barbarous cruelty.

Carthalo   Under correction,
             Give me leave to speak my thoughts. We are bound
                                              to weigh
             Not what we should do in the point of honour,
             Swayed by our pity, but what may be done
             With the safety of the state.

Asdrubal   Which is indeed
             The main consideration; for, grant
             This is the true Antiochus, without danger,
             Nay, almost certain ruin to ourselves,
             We cannot yield him favour or protection.

Hanno   We have feared and felt the Roman power, and must
             Expect, if we provoke him, a return
             Not limited to the quality of the offence.
             The tribute Rome receives from Asia is
             Her chief supportance; other provinces
             Hardly defray the charge by which they are
             Kept in subjection. They, in name perhaps,
             Render the Roman terrible, but his strength
             And power to do hurt without question is
             Derived from Asia. [This forfeited kingdom
             Binds the Empire's power in the East, it is
             Foundational to Rome. Should we in Carthage
             Lend our aid to one who'd undo this bind?
             Rome will pursue and punish us.]

Carthalo   I could wish
We were well rid of him.

Asdrubal   The surest course
Is to deliver him into the hands
Of bold Flaminius.

Hanno   And so oblige
Rome for a matchless benefit.

Amilcar   If my power
Were absolute – as 'tis but titular,
And that confined too, being by you elected
Prince of the Senate only for a year –
I would oppose your counsels, and not labour
With arguments to confute 'em. Yet, however,
Though a fellow patriot with you, let it not savour
Of usurpation, though in my opinion
I cross your abler judgements. Call to mind
With what expense of coin, as blood, our grandsires
Kept their liberty and maintained the scale
Of empire e'en 'twixt Carthage and proud Rome.
And though our Punic faith is branded by
Our enemies, our confederates and friends
Found it as firm as fate. Are seventeen kings
Our feodaries, our strengths upon the sea
Exceeding theirs, and our land soldiers
In number far above theirs? – though inferior
In arms, and discipline, to our shame we speak it.
And then for our cavalry in the campaign?
How often have they brake their piles and routed
Their coward legions?

Hanno   This I grant, sir, is not
To be contradicted.

Amilcar   This state hath been
The sanctuary to which mighty kings
Have fled to for protection, and found it.
Let it not to posterity be told
That we so far degenerate from the race
We are derived as, in a servile fear
Of the Roman power, we yielded up a man,

That wears the shape of our confederate,
To their devouring grip, whose strong assurance
Of our integrity and impartial doom
Hath made this seat his altar.

Carthalo   I join with you
In this opinion, but no farther than
It may be done with safety.

Asdrubal   In his ruins
To bury ourselves, you needs must grant to be
An inconsiderate pity no way suiting
With a wise man's reason.

Amilcar   (*To an Attendant*)   From the Senate
Entreat the Roman, Titus Flaminius,
To assist us with his counsel.

Hanno   And let the prisoner
Be brought into the court.

                                        Exit Attendant.

Amilcar   The gods of Carthage
Direct us to the right way.

                    Enter Flaminius.

Asdrubal   With what gravity
He does approach us.

Carthalo   As he would command,
Not argue, his desires.

Amilcar   May it please your lordship
To take your place?

Flaminius   In civil courtesy,
As I am Titus Flaminius, I may thank you.
But, sitting here as Rome's ambassador,
(In which you are honoured), to instruct you in
Her will, which you are bound to serve not argue,
I must not borrow – that were poor – but take
As a tribute due to her that's justly styled
The mistress of this earthly globe, the boldness

To reprehend your slow progression in
Doing her greatness right. That she believes,
In me, that this impostor was suborned
By the conquered Asiatics, in their hopes
Of future liberty, to usurp the name
Of dead Antiochus, should satisfy
Your scrupulous doubts, all proofs beyond this being
Merely superfluous.

Carthalo   My lord, my lord,
You trench too much upon us.

Asdrubal   We are not
Led by an implicit faith.

Hanno   Nor, though we would
Preserve Rome's amity, must not yield up
The freedom of our wills and judgements to
Quit or condemn as we shall be appointed
By her imperious pleasure.

Carthalo   We confess not,
Nor ever will, she hath a power above us.
Carthage is still her equal.

Amilcar   If you can
Prove this man an impostor, he shall suffer
As he deserves; if not, you shall perceive
You have no empire here.

Hanno   Call in the prisoner.
Then, as you please, confront him.

Flaminius   This neglect
Hereafter will be thought on.

Amilcar   We shall stand
The danger howsoever. When we did,
His cause unheard, at your request commit
This king, or this impostor, you received
More favour than we owed you.

Officer   (*Within*) Room for the prisoner.

Enter Officers, Antiochus, habited like a king,
Berecinthius, the three Merchants.

Antiochus   Health to the Senate.
We do suppose your duties done; sit still.
Titus Flaminius, we remember you.
As you are a public minister from Rome
You may sit.

Flaminius   How!

Antiochus   But as we are
A potent king, in whose court you have waited
And sought our favour, you betray your pride,
And the more than saucy rudeness of your manners.
A bended knee, remembering what we are,
Much better would become you.

Flaminius   Ha!

Antiochus   We said it,
But fall from our own height to hold discourse
With a thing so far beneath us.

Berecinthius   Admirable!

Amilcar   The Roman looks as he had seen the wolf!
How his confidence awes him.

Asdrubal   Be he what he will,
He bears himself like a king, and I must tell you
I am amazed too.

Antiochus   Are we so transformed
From what we were, since our disaster in
The Grecian enterprise, that you gaze upon us
As some strange prodigy never seen in Africa?
Antiochus speaks to you – the King Antiochus –
And challenges a retribution in
His entertainment of the love and favours
Extended to you. Call to memory
Your true friend and confederate, who refused,
In his respect to you, the proffered amity
Of the Roman people. Hath this vile enchanter
Environed me with such thick clouds in your

Erroneous belief, from his report
That I was long since dead, that, being present,
The beams of majesty cannot break through
The foggy mists raised by his wicked charms
To lend you light to know me? I cite you,
My lord Amilcar: now I look on you
As prince of the Senate, but, when you were less,
I have seen you in my court assisted by
Grave Hanno, Asdrubal, and Carthalo,
The pillars of the Carthaginian greatness.
I know you all. Antiochus ne'er deserved
To be thus slighted.

Amilcar   Not so. We in you
Look on the figure of the King Antiochus,
But without stronger proofs than yet you have
Produced to make us think so, cannot hear you
But as a man suspected.

Antiochus   Of what guilt?

Flaminius Of subornation, and imposture.

Antiochus   Silence
This fellow's saucy tongue! O majesty,
How soon a short eclipse hath made thy splendour,
As it had never shined on these, forgotten.
But you refuse to hear me as a king.
Deny not yet, in justice, what you grant
To common men – free liberty without
His interruption (having heard what he
Objects against me) to acquit myself
Of that which in his malice I am charged with.

Amilcar You have it.

Antiochus   As my present fortune wills me,
I thank your goodness. Rise, thou cursed agent
Of mischief, and accumulate in one heap
All engines by the devil thy tutor fashioned
To ruin innocence; in poison steep
Thy bloodied tongue and let thy words, as full
Of bitterness as malice, labour to

Seduce these noble hearers. Make me, in
Thy coinèd accusation, guilty of
Such crimes whose names my innocence ne'er knew,
I'll stand the charge; and when that thou hast shot
All arrows in thy quiver, feathered with
Slanders and aimed with cruelty, in vain,
My truth though yet concealed, the mountains of
Thy glossed fictions in her strength removed,
Shall in a glorious shape appear, and show
Thy painted mistress, Falsehood, when stripped bare
Of borrowed and adulterate colours, in
Her own shape and deformity.

Berecinthius   I am ravished!

1 Merchant O more than royal sir!

Amilcar   Forbear.

2 Merchant   The monster
Prepares to speak.

Berecinthius   And still that villainous smile
Ushers his following mischiefs.

Flaminius   Since the assurance
From one of my place, quality, and rank,
Is not sufficient with you to suppress
This bold seductor, to acquit our state
From the least tyrannous imputation,
I will forget awhile I am a Roman,
Whose arguments are warranted by his sword,
And not filed from his tongue. This creature here,
That styles himself Antiochus, I know
For an apostate Jew, though others say
He is a cheating Greek called Pseudolus,
And keeps a whore in Corinth. But I'll come
To real proofs, reports and rumours being
Subjects unsuitable with my gravity
To speak, or yours to hear. 'Tis most apparent
The king Antiochus was slain in Greece,
His body at his subjects' suit delivered,

His ashes from the funeral pile raked up
And in a golden urn preserved, and kept
In the royal monument of the Asian kings.
Such was the clemency of Marcus Scaurus,
The Roman conqueror, whose triumph was
Graced only with his statue. But suppose
He had survived – which is impossible.
Can it fall in the compass of your reason
That this impostor – if he were the man
Which he with impudence affirms he is –
Would have wandered two and twenty tedious years
Like a vagabond o'er the world, and not have tried
Rome's mercy as a suppliant?
All ages have been furnished
With such as have usurped upon the names
And persons of dead princes. Is it not
As evident as the day this wretch, instructed
By these poor Asians (sworn enemies
To the majesty of Rome) but personates
The dead Antiochus, hired to it by these
To stir up a rebellion, which they call
Delivery or restoring?

Antiochus   Would I were dead indeed,
Rather than hear this living.

Flaminius   I confess
He hath some marks of King Antiochus, but
The most of 'em artificial. Then observe
What kind of men they are that do abet him:
Proscribed and banished persons, the ringleader
Of this seditious troop a turbulent flamen
Grown fat with idleness –

Berecinthius   That's I!

Flaminius   And puffed up
With the wind of his ambition.

Berecinthius   With reverence to
The state, thou liest. [Were my will not so
Sheathed in this bulk, would I] deflower thy sister.

Amilcar   Thank your goddess. She
               Defends you from a whipping.

Hanno   Take him off,
               He does disturb the court.

Berecinthius   I shall find a place yet
               Where I will roar my wrongs out.

                                    Exeunt Officers with Berecinthius.

Flaminius   As you have,
               In the removing of that violent fool,
               Given me a taste of your severity,
               Make it a feast, and perfect your great justice
               In the surrendering up this false pretender
               To the correction of the law.

Antiochus   As you wish
               A noble memory to aftertimes,
               Reserve one ear for my defence, and let not –
               For your own wisdoms, let not – that belief
               This subtle fiend would plant be rooted in you
               Till you have heard me. Would you know the truth
               And real cause why poor Antiochus hath
               So long concealed himself? Though in the opening
               A wound, in some degree by time closed up,
               I shall pour scalding oil and sulphur in it,
               I will, in the relation of my
               To-be-lamented story, punctually
               Confute my false accuser. Pray you conceive,
               As far as your compassion will permit,
               How great the grief and agony of my soul was
               When I considered that the violence
               Of my ill-reined ambition had made Greece
               The fatal sepulchre of so many thousands
               Of brave and able men that might have stood
               In opposition for the defence
               Of mine own kingdom, and a ready aid
               For my confederates. After which rout,
               And my retreat in a disguise to Corinth,
               The shame of this disgrace would have deterred me

                  From being ever seen where I was known.
                  And such was then my resolution.

Amilcar   This granted, whither went you?

Antiochus   As a punishment
                  Imposed upon myself, and equal to
                  My wilful folly, giving o'er the world
                  I went into a desert.

Flaminius   (*Aside*)   This agrees
                  With the dead slaves' report, but I must contemn it.

Amilcar   What drew you from that austere life?

Asdrubal   Clear that.

Antiochus   The counsel of a grave philosopher
                  Wrought on me to make known myself the man
                  That I was born, and of all potentates
                  In Africa to determine of the truth
                  Of my life and condition, I preferred
                  The commonwealth of Carthage.

Flaminius   As the fittest
                  To be abused.

Antiochus   This is not fair.

Amilcar   (*To Flaminius*)   My lord,
                  If not entreat, I must command your silence
                  Or absence, which you please.

Flaminius   So peremptory.

Antiochus   (*Produces a scroll*)
                  To vindicate myself from all suspicion
                  Of forgery and imposture, in this scroll,
                  Writ with my royal hand, you may peruse
                  A true memorial of all circumstances,
                  Answers, despatches, doubts, and difficulties,
                  Between myself and your ambassadors
                  Sent to negotiate with me.

Amilcar   Fetch the records.

                                Exit Officer.

Antiochus   'Tis my desire you should. Truth seeks the light.
And, when you have compared 'em, if you find 'em
In any point of moment differing,
Conclude me such a one as this false man
Presents me to you. Now for my death,
The firmest base on which he builds the strength
Of his assertions: if you please to weigh it
With your accustomed wisdom, you'll perceive
'Tis merely fabulous. Why did Rome not
Suffer the carcass they affirmed was mine
To be viewed by men that were bred up with me
And were familiar with the marks I carried
Upon my body, and not rely upon
Poor prisoners taken in the war, from whom,
In hope of liberty and reward, they drew
Such depositions as they knew would make
For their dark ends? Was anything more easy
Than to suppose a body, and that placed on
A solemn hearse, with funeral pomp to inter it
In a rich monument, and then proclaim
'This is the body of Antiochus,
King of the Lower Asia'?

Flaminius   Rome's honour
Is taxed in this of practice and corruption;
I'll hear no more. In your determinations,
Consider what it is to hold and keep her
Your friend or enemy.

                                    Exit Flaminius.

Amilcar   We wish we could
Receive you as a king, since your relation
Hath wrought so much upon us that we do
Incline to that belief. But since we cannot
As such protect you but with certain danger,
Until you are by other potent nations
Proclaimed for such, our fitting caution
Cannot be censured, though we do entreat
You would elsewhere seek justice.

Antiochus   Where, when 'tis
Frighted from you by power?

Amilcar   And yet take comfort:
Not all the threats of Rome shall force us to
Deliver you. The short time that you stay
In Carthage you are safe. No more a prisoner;
You are enlarged. With full security
Consult of your affairs. In what we may
We are your friends. Break up the court.

                          Exeunt Carthaginians.

1 Merchant   Dear sir,
Take courage in your liberty. The world
Lies open to you.

2 Merchant   We shall meet with comfort
When most despaired of by us.

Antiochus   Never. Never.
Poor men though fallen may rise, but kings like me
If once by fortune slaved, are ne'er set free.

                          Exeunt.

ACT THREE

SCENE ONE

Enter Flaminius (with two letters), Calistus and Demetrius.

Flaminius	You gave her store of gold with the instructions That I prescribed her?
Calistus	Yes, my lord, and on The forfeiture of my credit with your honour, Tajah will do her parts and dive into Their deepest secrets.
Flaminius	Men of place pay dear For their intelligence; it eats out the profit Of their employment. But in a design Of such weight, prodigality is a virtue. The fellow was of trust that you despatched To Rome with the packet?
Demetrius	Yes, sir; he flies, not rides. By this, if his access answer his care, He is upon return.
Flaminius	I am on the stage, And, if now, in the scene imposed upon me, So full of change – nay a mere labyrinth Of politic windings – I show not myself A protean actor, varying every shape With the occasion, it will hardly poise The expectation. I'll so place my nets That, if this bird want wings to carry him At one flight out of Africa, I shall catch him. Calistus.
Calistus	Sir.
Flaminius	(*Giving letters*) Give these at Syracuse To the proconsul Marcellus. Let another post

To Sardinia with these. – You have the picture
Of the impostor?

Demetrius   Drawn to the life, my lord.

Flaminius   Take it along with you. I have commanded,
In the Senate's name, that they man out their galleys,
And not to let one vessel pass without
A strict examination. The sea
Shall not protect him from me.

Lentulus   (*Within*)   I will excuse
My visit without preparation, fear not.

Enter Lentulus.

Flaminius   Who have we here?

Lentulus   When you have viewed me better
You will resolve yourself.

Flaminius   My good Lord Lentulus.

Lentulus   You name me right. The speed that brought me hither
As you see accoutred, and without a train
Suitable to my rank, may tell your lordship
That the design admits no vacant time
For compliment. Your advertisements have been read
In open court. The consuls and the Senate
Are full of wonder and astonishment
At the relation. Your care is much
Commended, and will find a due reward
When what you have so well begun is ended.
In the meantime, with their particular thanks,
They thus salute you.
(*Hands over a letter*)   You shall find there that –
Their good opinion of me far above
My hopes or merits – they have appointed me
Your successor in Carthage, and commit
Unto your abler trust the prosecution
Of this impostor.

Flaminius   As their creature ever
I shall obey, and serve 'em. I will leave

My freedman to instruct you in the course
Of my proceedings. You shall find him able
And faithful, on my honour.

Lentulus   I receive him
At his due value. Can you guess yet whither
This creature tends? By some passengers I met
I was told, howe'er the state denies to yield him
To our dispose, they will not yet incense us
By giving him protection.

Flaminius   Ere long
I hope I shall resolve you.

Enter Tajah.

                                   To my wish,
Here comes my true discoverer. Be brief,
And labour not with circumstance to endear
The service thou hast done me.

Tajah   As your lordship
Commanded me, in this Carthaginian habit
I made my first approaches, and delivered
The gold was given me as a private present
Sent from the lord Amilcar, for his viaticum
To another country, for I did pretend
I was his menial servant.

Flaminius   Very well.

Tajah   'Twas entertained almost with sacrifice,
And I, as one most welcome, was admitted
Into their turbulent council. Many means
Were there propounded, whither, and to whom,
Their King Antiochus (for so they style him)
Should fly for safety. But, in conclusion,
The corpulent flamen, that would govern all,
And in his nature would not give allowance
To any proposition that was not
The child of his own brain, resolved to carry
Their May-game prince, covered with a disguise,
To Prusias, King of Bithynia. His opinion
Carried it, and thither they are gone

Upon my certain knowledge, for I rid
Two days and nights along, that I might not build
Upon suppositions. By this they are
At their journey's end.

Flaminius   (*Gives money*) With my thanks there's thy reward.
I will take little rest until I have
Soured his sweet entertainment. – You have been
In the court of this Prusias. Of what temper is he?

Lentulus   A well-disposed and noble gentleman,
And very careful to preserve the peace
And quiet of his subjects.

Flaminius   I shall find him
The apter to be wrought on. Do you know who is
His special favourite?

Lentulus   One that was his tutor.
A seeming politician, and talks often
The end of his ambition is to be
A gentleman of Rome.

Flaminius   I shall fit him, fear not.
Your travail's ended. Mine begins, and therefore
Sans ceremony I will take my leave.
Formality of manners now is useless;
I long to be a-horseback.

Lentulus   You have my wishes
For a fair success.

Flaminius   My care shall not be wanting.

                                                            Exeunt.

SCENE TWO

Enter Antiochus and the three Merchants.

1 Merchant   This tedious journey, from your majesty's
Long discontinuance of riding hard,
With weariness hath dulled your spirits.

2 Merchant   The flamen,
His corpulency considered, hath held out
Beyond imagination.

3 Merchant   As often
As he rode down a hill I did expect
The chining of his horse.

Antiochus   I wonder more
How mine sustained his burden, since the weight
That sits on my more heavy heart would crack
The sinews of an elephant.

1 Merchant   O part not, sir,
From your own strength by yielding to despair.
I am most confident Berecinthius will,
From the great King Prusias – in his goodness great –
Bring comfort to you.

Antiochus   I am prepared, however.
Lower I cannot fall.

                                              Flourish.

3 Merchant   Ha! These are signs
Of a glorious entertainment, not contempt.

                        Enter Berecinthius.

Berecinthius Bear up, sir. I have done you simple service,
I thank my eloquence and boldness for it.
O, for a dozen of rubbers and a bath.
And yet I need no tub, since I drench myself
In mine own balsam.

1 Merchant   Balsam? It smells
Like a tallow-chandler's shop.

Berecinthius   Does it so, you thin-gut?
Thou thing without moisture! But I have no time
To answer thee.
(*To Antiochus*)   The great king – by my means, sir,
Ever remember that – in his own person,
With his fair consort and a gallant train,
Are come to entertain you.

Antiochus   Jove, if thou art
            Pleased that it shall be so –

Berecinthius   Change not you Jove's purpose
            In your slowness to receive it. In your carriage
            Express yourself. They come.

Enter Prusias, King of Bithynia, the Queen of Bithynia,
Philoxenus, with Attendants.

Prusias   The strong assurance
            You gave at Carthage to confirm you are
            The King Antiochus (for so much from
            My agent there I have heard) commands me to
            Believe you are so. And however they,
            Awed by the Roman greatness, durst not lend you
            Aid or protection, in me you shall find
            A surer guard: I stand on mine own bases.
            Nor shall or threats or prayers deter me from
            Doing a good deed in itself rewarded.
            You are welcome to my bosom.

Antiochus   All that yet
            I can return you, sir, is thanks, expressed
            In tears of joy, to find here that compassion
            Hath not forsook the earth.

Queen   Alas, good king,
            I pity him.

Prusias   This lady, sir, your servant,
            Presents her duty to you.

Antiochus   Pray you forgive me.
            Calamity, my too long rude companion,
            Hath taught me, gracious madam, to forget
            Civility and manners.   *Kisses her.*

Queen   (*Aside*)   I ne'er touched
            But the king my husband's lips, and as I live,
            He kisses very like him.

Prusias   Here is one
            I dare present to you for a knowing man

In politic designs. But he is present,
I should say more else.

Antiochus   Your assistance, sir,
To raise a trod-down king, will well become you.

Philoxenus   What man can do that is familiar with
The deep directions of Xenophon,
Or Aristotle's *Politics*, besides
Mine own collections – which some prefer,
And with good reason, as they say, before 'em –
Your highness may expect.

Prusias   We will at leisure
Consider of the manner and the means
How to restore you to your own.

Queen   And till then
Suppose yourself in your own court.

Antiochus   The gods
Be sureties for the payment of this debt
I stand engaged. Your bounties overwhelm me.

Exeunt Prusias, Antiochus, the Queen, Philoxenus and Attendants.

Berecinthius   Ay, marry, this is as it should be, ha?
After these storms raised by this Roman devil,
Titus Flaminius – you know whom I mean –
Are we got into the port once. I must purge.

1 Merchant   Not without cause.

Berecinthius   Or my increasing belly
Will metamorphose me into the shape
Of a great tortoise, and I shall appear
A cipher, a round man, or what you will.
Now jeer at my bulk and spare not.

1 Merchant   You are pleasant.

Berecinthius   Farce thy lean ribs with hope, and thou wilt grow to
Another kind of creature. When our king is
Restored, let me consider, as he must be,
And I the principal means, I'll first grow rich,
Infinite rich, and build a strange new temple

To the goddess that I worship, and so bind her
To prosper all my purposes.

2 Merchant   Be not rapt so.

Berecinthius Prithee do not trouble me. First I will expel
The Romans out of Asia; and so, breaking
Their reputation in the world, we will
Renew our league with Carthage, then draw into
Our party the Egyptian Ptolemy,
And great Arsaces' issue. I will be
The general, and march to Rome, which taken,
I'll fill proud Tiber with the carcasses
Of men, women and children. Do not persuade me!
I'll show no mercy.

3 Merchant   Have the power to hurt first.

Berecinthius Then by the senators, whom I'll use as horses,
I will be drawn in a chariot, made for my bulk,
In triumph to the Capitol, more admired
Than Bacchus was in India. Titus Flaminius,
Our enemy, led like a dog in a chain,
As I descend, or reascend, in state,
Shall serve for my footstool. I will conjure him,
If revenge hath any spells.

Enter Flaminius and Demetrius.

Flaminius   Command the captain
To wait me with his galley at the next port.
I am confident I shall freight him.

Exit Demetrius.

1 Merchant   You are conjuring
And see what you have raised.

Berecinthius   Cybele save me!
I do not fear thee, Pluto, though thou hast
Assumed a shape not to be matched in Cocytus.
Why dost thou follow me?

Flaminius   Art thou mad?

Berecinthius   Thou com'st

To make me so. How my jelly quakes! Avaunt.
What have I to do with thee?

Flaminius   You shall know at leisure.
The time is now too precious.

                                                        Exit Flaminius.

Berecinthius   'Tis vanished!
Sure, 'twas an apparition.

1 Merchant   I fear
A fatal one to us.

2 Merchant   We may easily guess at
The cause that brings him hither.

2 Merchant   Now, if ever,
Confirm the king.

1 Merchant   Against this battery
New works are to be raised, or we are ruined.

Berecinthius What think you of this rampart? 'Twill hold out,
And he shall shoot through and through it, but I'll
                                                cross him.

                                                        Exeunt.

SCENE THREE

Enter Flaminius and Philoxenus.

Flaminius   What we have said the consuls will make good,
And the glad Senate ratify.

Philoxenus   They have so
Obliged me for this favour, that there is not
A service of that difficulty from which
I would decline. In this rest confident.
I am your own, and sure.

Flaminius   You shall do, sir,
A noble office in it; and however

We thank you for the courtesy, the profit
And certain honours, the world's terror, Rome,
In thankfulness cannot but shower upon you,
Are wholly yours. How happy I esteem
Myself, in this employment, to meet with
A wise and provident statesman.

Philoxenus   My good lord.

Flaminius   I flatter not in speaking truth. You are so,
And in this prompt alacrity confirm it,
Since a wise forecast in the managing
Worldly affairs is the true wisdom, rashness
The schoolmistress of idiots. You well know
Charity begins at home, and that we are
Nearest unto ourselves. Fools build upon
Imaginary hopes, but wise men ever
On real certainties. As you are a statesman,
And a master in that art, you must remove
All rubs, though with a little wrong sometimes,
That may put by the bias of your counsels
From the fair mark they aim at.

Philoxenus You are read well in worldly passages.

Flaminius   I barter with you such trifles as I have;
But to the point. With speed get me access
To the king, your pupil, and 'tis well for him
That he hath such a tutor. Rich Bithynia
Was never so indebted to a patriot
And vigilant watchman for her peace and safety
As to yourself.

Philoxenus   Without boast I may whisper
I have done something that way.

Flaminius   Truth proclaims it.
But when it shall be understood you are
The principal means by which a dangerous serpent,
Warmed in your sovereign's bosom, is delivered,
To have his sting and venomous teeth pulled out,
Not Prusias alone, but his saved people,
Will raise your providence altars.

Philoxenus   Let me entreat
Your patience some few minutes, I'll bring the king
In person to you.

Flaminius   Do, and this effected,
Think of the ring you are privileged to wear
When a Roman gentleman, and, after that,
Of provinces – and purple.

                                    Exit Philoxenus.

                                    I must smile now
In my consideration with what glibness
My flatteries, oiled with hopes of future greatness,
Are swallowed by this dull pate. But it is not
Worth th'observation – most of our seeming statesmen
Are caught in the same noose.

          Enter Prusias and Philoxenus.

(*Aside*)   Returned so soon,
And the king with him. No matter; I am for him.

Prusias   From the people of Rome? So quick! What can he
Propound which I must fear to hear? I would
Continue in fair terms with that warlike nation,
Ever provided I wrong not myself
In the least point of honour.

Philoxenus   To the full
He will instruct your majesty.

Flaminius   So may
Felicity, as a page, attend your person,
As you embrace the friendly counsel sent you
From the Roman Senate.

Prusias   With my thanks to you,
Their instrument, if the advice be such
As by this preparation you would have me
Conceive it is, I shall, and 'twill become me,
Receive it as a favour.

Flaminius   Know then, Rome,

In her pious care that you may still increase
The happiness you live in, and your subjects,
Under the shadow of their own vines, eat
The fruit they yield 'em, their soft musical feasts
Continuing as they do yet, unaffrighted
With the harsh noise of war, entreats as low
As her known power and majesty can descend,
You would return, with due equality,
A willingness to preserve what she hath conquered
From change and innovation.

Prusias   I attempt not
To trouble her, nor ever will.

Flaminius   ·   Fix there.
Or if, for your own good, you will move farther,
Make Rome your thankful debtor by surrendering
Into her hands the false impostor that
Seeks to disturb her quiet.

Prusias   This I looked for,
And that I should find mortal poison wrapped up
In your candied pills. Must I, because you say so,
Believe that this most miserable king is
A false affronter who, with arguments
Unanswerable and mere miraculous proofs,
Confirms himself the true Antiochus?
Or is it not sufficient that you Romans,
In your unsatisfied ambition, have
Seized with an unjust grip on half the world,
Which you call conquest, if that I consent not
To have my innocence soiled with that pollution
You are willingly smeared o'er with –

Flaminius   Pray you hear me.

Prusias   I will be first heard. Shall I, for your ends,
Infringe my princely word, or break the laws
Of hospitality? Defeat myself
Of the certain honour to restore a king
Unto his own, and what you Romans have
Extorted and keep from him? Far be it from me.
I will not buy your amity at such loss,

So it be to all aftertimes remembered
I held it not sufficient to live
As one born only for myself, and I
Desire no other monument.

Flaminius   Your inclination
Is honourable, but your power deficient
To put your purposes into act.

Prusias   My power?

Flaminius   Is not to be disputed if weighed truly
With the petty kings your neighbours, but when
                                          balanced
With the globes and sceptres of my mistress, Rome,
Will – but I spare comparisons.
You keep in pay, 'tis true, some peace-trained troops
Which awe your neighbours. But consider, when
Our eagles shall display their sail-stretched wings,
Hovering o'er our legions, what defence
Can you expect from yours?

Philoxenus   Urge that point home.

Flaminius   Our old victorious bands are ever ready,
And such as are not our confederates tremble
To think where next the storm shall fall with horror.
Philoxenus knows it. Will you, to help one
You should condemn, and is not worth your pity,
Pull it on your own head? Your neighbour, Carthage,
Would smile to see your error. Let me paint
The danger to you ere it come: imagine
Our legions, and th'auxiliary forces
Of such as are our friends and tributaries,
Drawn up; Bithynia covered with our armies;
All places promising defence blocked up
With our armed troops; the siege continuing;
Famine within and force without disabling
All opposition; then, the army entered,
As victory is insolent, the rapes
Of virgins and grave matrons; reverend old men
With their last groans accusing you; your city
And palace sacked –

Philoxenus	Dear sir –

Flaminius   And you yourself
Captived, and, after that, chained by the neck;
Your matchless queen, your children, officers, friends,
Waiting as scorns of fortune to give lustre
To the victor's triumph.

Philoxenus   I am in a fever to think upon 't.

Flaminius   As a friend I have delivered –
And more than my commission warrants me –
This caution to you. But now: peace or war?
If the first, I entertain it; if the latter
I'll instantly defy you.

Philoxenus   Pray you say peace, sir.

Prusias   On what conditions?

Flaminius   The delivery
Of this seductor and his complices;
On no terms else, and suddenly.

Prusias   How can I
Dispense with my faith given?

Philoxenus   I'll yield you reasons.

Prusias   Let it be peace then. O, pray you, call in
The wretched man. In the meantime I'll consider
How to excuse myself.

                                    Exit Philoxenus.

Flaminius   (*Aside*)   While I in silence
Triumph in my success, and meditate
On the reward that crowns it. A strong army
Could have done no more than I alone, and with
A little breath, have effected.

*Enter Antiochus, the Queen, Philoxenus, Berecinthius,
the Merchants, Demetrius.*

Antiochus   Goodness guard me!
Whom do I look on? Sir, come further from him;
He is infectious. If you hear him,

There is no touch of moral honesty,
Though rampired in your soul, but will fly from you.
The mandrake's shrieks, the aspic's deadly tooth,
The tears of crocodiles or the basilisk's eye
Kill not so soon, nor with that violence,
As he who in his cruel nature holds
Antipathy with mercy.

Prusias   I am sorry.

Antiochus Sorry? For what? That you had an intent
To be a good and just prince? Are compassion
And charity grown crimes?

Prusias   The gods can witness
How much I would do for you. And but that
Necessity of state –

Antiochus   Make not the gods
Guilty of your breach of faith; from them you find not
Treachery commanded. And the state that seeks
Strength from disloyalty, in the quicksands which
She trusteth in is swallowed. 'Tis in vain
To argue with you. If I am condemned,
Defences come too late. What do you purpose
Shall fall on poor Antiochus?

Prusias   For my
Security – there being no means left else –
Against my will I must deliver you.

Antiochus   To whom?

Prusias To Rome's ambassador.

Antiochus   O the furies
Exceed not him in cruelty. Remember
I am a king. Your royal guest. Your right hand
The pawn and pledge that should defend me from
My bloody enemy. Did you accuse
The Carthaginian Senate for denying
Aid and protection to me, giving hope
To my despairing fortunes? And will you now
So far transcend them in a coward fear,

Declaimed against by your own mouth? O sir,
If you dare not give me harbour, set me safe yet
In any desert, where this serpent's hisses
May not be heard, and to the gods I'll speak you
A prince both wise and honourable.

Prusias   Alas, it is not in my power.

Antiochus   As an impostor
Take off my head then; at the least so far
Prove merciful, or with any torture ease me
Of the burden of a life, rather than yield me
To this politic state hangman.

Flaminius   (*Aside*)   This to me is
A kind of ravishing music.

Queen   I have lived
For many years, sir, your obedient handmaid,
Nor ever in a syllable presumed
To cross your purposes. But now, with a sorrow
As great almost as this poor king's, beholding
Your poverty of spirit – for it does
Deserve no better name – I must put off
Obsequiousness and silence, and take to me
The warrant and authority of your queen,
And as such give you counsel.

Prusias   You displease me.

Queen   The physic promising health is ever bitter.
Hear me. Will you that are a man – nay, more,
A king of men – do that, forced to it by fear,
Which common men would scorn? I am a woman,
A weak and feeble woman, yet before
I would deliver up my bondwoman,
And have it told I did it by constraint,
I would endure to have these hands cut off,
These eyes pulled out –

Prusias   I'll hear no more.

Queen   Do you, then,
As a king should.

Prusias   Away with her.

                              They bear off the Queen.

Flaminius   My affairs
Exact a quick despatch.

Prusias   He's yours. Conceive
What I would say. Farewell.

                              Exeunt Prusias and Philoxenus.

Antiochus   That I had been
Born dumb. I will not grace thy triumph, tyrant,
With one request of favour.

                              Exit Antiochus, guarded.

Berecinthius   My good lord.

Flaminius   Your will, dear flamen?

Berecinthius   I perceive you are like
To draw a great charge upon you. My fat bulk,
And these my lions, will not be kept for a little,
Nor would we be chargeable. And therefore, kissing
Your honoured hands, I take my leave.

Flaminius   By no means.
I have been busy, but I shall find leisure
To treat with you in another place.

Berecinthius   I would not
Put your lordship to the trouble.

Flaminius   It will be
A pleasure rather. Bring 'em all away.

Berecinthius   The comfort is, whether I drown or hang
I shall not be long about it. I'll preserve
The dignity of my family.

Flaminius   'Twill become you.

                              Exeunt.

ACT FOUR

SCENE ONE

Enter Metellus (a Proconsul of Lusitania),
and Sempronius (a Centurion).

Metellus	A revolt in Asia?

Sempronius Yes, on the report
The long-thought-dead Antiochus lives.

Metellus I heard
Such a one appeared in Carthage, but suppressed
By Titus Flaminius, my noble friend,
Who by his letters promised me a visit,
If his designs – as I desire they may –
Succeeded to his wishes.

Sempronius Till you behold him,
I can bring your honour, if you please, where you
May find fair entertainment.

Metellus From whom, captain?

Sempronius A new-rigged pinnace that put off from Corinth,
And is arrived among us, tight and yare.
Nor comes she to pay custom for her freight,
But to impose a tax on such as dare
Presume to look on her, which smock-gamesters offer
Sooner than she demands it.

Metellus Some fresh courtesan,
Upon mine honour.

Sempronius You are i'the right, my lord.

Metellus And there lies your intelligence?

Sempronius True, my good lord;
'Tis a discovery will not shame a captain
When he lies in garrison. Since I was a trader

In such commodities I never saw
Her equal. I was ravished with the object,
And would you visit her I believe you would write
Yourself of my opinion.

Metellus   Fie upon thee!
I am old.

Sempronius   And therefore have the greater use
Of such a cordial. All Medea's drugs,
And her charms to boot, were nothing to her touch.
She hath done miracles since she came: a usurer,
Full of the gout and more diseases than
His crutches could support, used her rare physic
But one short night and, rising in the morning,
He danced a lavolta.

Metellus   Prithee, leave thy fooling,
And talk of something else.

Sempronius   The whole world yields not
Apter discourse. She hath all the qualities
Conducing to the sport: sings like a siren,
Dances as the gross element of earth
Had no part in her, her discourse so full
Of eloquence and prevailing, there is nothing
She asks to be denied her. Had she desired
My captain's place I had cashiered myself,
And should she beg your proconsulship, if you heard
                                                              her,
'Twere hers, upon my life.

Enter Flaminius.

Metellus   She should be damned first,
And her whole tribe. – My lord Flaminius, welcome.
I have long been full of expectation
Of your great design, and hope a fair success
Hath crowned your travail, in your bringing in
This dangerous impostor.

Flaminius   At the length,
I have him, and his complices.

Metellus	I'll not now
	Inquire how you achieved him, but would know –
	Since 'tis referred to you – what punishment
	Shall fall upon him.

Flaminius   If you please, in private
I will acquaint you.

Metellus   Captain, let me entreat you
To meditate on your woman in the next room;
We may have employment for you.

Sempronius   I had rather
She would command my service.

Exit Sempronius.

Metellus   Pray you, sit.

Flaminius Now, my good lord, I ask your grave advice
What course to take.

Metellus   That, in my judgement, needs not
Long consultation. He is a traitor,
And, his process framed, must as a traitor suffer
A death due to his treason.

Flaminius   There's much more
To be considered, there being a belief
Dispersed almost through Asia that he is
The true Antiochus. And we must decline
The certain scandal it will draw upon
The Roman government if he die the man
He is by the most received to be. And therefore,
Till that opinion be removed, we must
Use some quaint practice, that may work upon
His hopes or fears, to draw a free confession
That he was suborned to take on him the name
He still maintains.

Metellus   That, torture will wrest from him;
I know no readier way.

Flaminius   If you had seen
His carriage in Carthage and Bithynia
You would not think so. Since I had him in

My power I have used all possible means that might
Force him into despair and so to do
A violence on himself. He hath not tasted
These three days any sustenance, and still
Continues fasting.

Metellus   Keep him to that diet
Some few hours more.

Flaminius   I am of opinion rather,
Some competence offered him, and a place of rest
Where he might spend the remnant of his days
In pleasure and security, might do more
Than fear of death or torture.

Metellus   It may be
There are such natures; and now I think upon't,
I can help you to a happy instrument
To motion it. Your ear.   *Whispers.*

Flaminius   'Tis wondrous well,
And it may prove fortunate.

Metellus   'Tis but a trial.
However, I will send for her.

Flaminius   Pray you do.
She shall have my directions.

Metellus   What botches
Are made in the shop of policy.

Flaminius   So they cover
The nakedness we must conceal, it skills not.

                                             Exeunt.

SCENE TWO

Enter Antiochus and Jailer, with a dagger and a noose.

Jailer   (*Aside*) Why should I feel compunction for that
             Which yields me profit, ha? A prisoner's tears

Should sooner pierce flint or Egyptian marble
Than move us to compassion. Yet I know not,
The sufferings of this miserable man
Work strangely on me. Some say he is a king.
It may be so, but if they hold out thus
I am sure he is like to die a beggar's death
And starve for hunger. I am by a servant
Of the lord Flaminius strictly commanded,
Before I have raised him out of the dungeon,
To lay these instruments in his view, to what end
I am not to inquire, but I am certain
After his long fast they are viands that
Will hardly be digested. (*To Antiochus*) Do you hear, sir?

Antiochus   If thou art my deathsman, welcome.

Jailer   I so pity you
That I wish I had commission, as you rise,
To free you from all future misery,
To knock your brains out.

Antiochus   Would thou hadst.

Jailer   You have
The liberty to air yourself, and that
Is all I can afford you. Fast and be merry,
I am elsewhere called on.

                                        Exit Jailer.

Antiochus   Death – as far as faintness
Will give me leave to chide thee – I am angry
Thou com'st not at me. No attendance? Famine,
Thy meagre harbinger, flatters me with hope
Of thy so wished arrival, yet thy coming
Is still deferred. Why? Is it in thy scorn
To take a lodging here? I am a king,
And though I know the reverence that waits
Upon the potent sceptre, nor the guards
Of faithful subjects, neither threats nor prayers
Of friends or kindred, nor yet walls of brass
Or fire, should their proud height knock at the moon,
Can stop thy passage when thou art resolved

To force thy entrance. Yet a king, in reason,
By the will of fate severed from common men,
Should have the privilege and prerogative,
When he is willing to disrobe himself
Of this cobweb garment – life – to have thee ready
To do thy fatal office. What have we here?

Enter Metellus, Flaminius, Sempronius, above.

A poniard and a halter. From the objects
I am easily instructed to what end
They were prepared. Either will serve the turn
To ease the burthen of a wretched life
Or thus (*the dagger*), or thus (*the noose*). In death
                       I must commend
The Roman courtesy. How am I grown
So cheap and vile in their opinion that
I am denied an executioner?
Will not the loss of my life quit the cost?
O rare frugality. Will they force me to
Be mine own hangman? Every slave that's guilty
Of crimes not to be named receives such favour
By the judge's doom. And is my innocence –
The oppressed innocence of a star-crossed king –
Held more contemptible? My better angel,
Though wanting power to alter fate, discovers
Their hellish purposes. Yes, yes, 'tis so.
My body's death will not suffice, they aimed at
My soul's perdition; and shall I, to shun
A few hours more of misery, betray her?
No, she is free still, and shall so return
From whence she came, and in her pureness triumph,
Their tyranny chained and fettered.

Flaminius
                                  I pine with envy
To see his constancy.

Metellus
                    Bid your property enter
And use her subtlest magic.

Sempronius
                  I have already
Acquainted her with her cue. The music ushers
Her personal appearance.

Music and a song.

Antiochus   From what hand
And voice do I receive this charity?
But I miscall it.

Enter Courtesan.

                                          'Tis some new-found engine
Mounted to batter me. Ha!

Courtesan   If I were not
More harsh and rugged in my disposition
Than thy tormentors, these eyes had outstripped
My tongue, and with a shower of tears had told you
Compassion brings me hither.

Antiochus   That I could
Believe so much, as by my miseries –
An oath I dare not break – I gladly would.
Pity, methinks I know not how, appears
So lovely in you.

Courtesan   It being spent upon
A subject in each circumstance deserving
An universal sorrow, though 'tis simple,
It cannot be deformed. May I presume
To kiss your royal hand, for sure you are not
Less than a king.

Antiochus   Have I one witness living
Dares only think so much?

Courtesan   I do believe it,
And will die in that belief; and nothing more
Confirms it than your patience, not to be
Found in a meaner man. Not all the trim
Of the majesty you were born to, though set off
With pomp and glorious lustre, showed you in
Such full perfection as at this instant
Shines round about you, in your constant bearing
Your adverse fortune a degree beyond
All magnanimity that ever was
Canonised by mankind.

Antiochus   Astonishment
And wonder seizes on me. Pray you, what are you?

Courtesan   Without your pity, nearer to the grave
Than the malice of prevailing enemies
Can hurry you.

Antiochus   My pity! I will part with
So much from what I have engrossed to mourn
Mine own afflictions, as I freely grant it.
Will you have me weep before I know the cause
In which I may serve you?

Courtesan   You already have
Spent too much of that stock. Pray you, first hear me,
And wrong not my simplicity with doubts
Of that I shall deliver. I am a virgin –

Sempronius If I had not toyed with her myself I should now
believe her.

Courtesan   And though not of the eagle's brood, descended
From a noble family.

Sempronius   Her mother sold her
To a Corinthian lecher at thirteen,
As 'tis reported.

Metullus   Be silent, I command you!

Antiochus   To be a virgin, and so well derived,
In my opinion, fair one, are not things
To be lamented.

Courtesan   If I had not fallen
From my clear height of chastity – I confess it –
In my too forward wishes, and that is
A sin I am guilty of. I am in love, sir,
Impotently mad in love, and my desires
Not to be stopped in their career.

Antiochus   With whom
Are you so taken?

Courtesan   With your own dear self, sir.
Behold me not with such a face of wonder.

It is too sad a truth. The story of
Your most deplorable fortune at the first warmed me
With more then modest heats, but since I saw you
I am all fire, and shall turn cinders if
You show not mercy to me.

Antiochus   Foolish creature.
If I could suppose this true, and met your wishes
With equal ardour, as I am, what shadow
Of seeming hope is left you to arrive at
The port you long for?

Courtesan   If you will be good
Unto yourself, the voyage is accomplished.
It is but putting off a poisoned shirt,
Which in the wearing eats into your flesh.

Antiochus   Clear this dark mystery, for yet to me
You speak in riddles.

Courtesan   I will make it easy
To your understanding, and thus sweeten it
In the delivery. (*Offers to kiss him*) 'Tis but to disclaim,
With the continual cares that wait upon it,
The title of a king.

Antiochus   (*Aside*)   Devil Flaminius!
I find you here.

Courtesan   Why do you turn away?
The counsel that I offer, if you please
To entertain it, brings liberty and a calm
After so many storms. And you no sooner
Shall to the world profess you were suborned
To this imposture – though I still believe
It is a truth – but, with a free remission
For the offence, I, as your better genius,
Will lead you from this place of horror to
A paradise of delight, to which compared,
Thessalian Tempe, or that garden where
Venus with her revived Adonis spend
Their pleasant hours and make from their embraces
A perpetuity of happiness,

Deserve not to be named. There, in an arbour,
Of itself supported o'er a bubbling spring,
With purple hyacinths and roses covered,
We will enjoy the sweets of life. Nor shall
Arithmetic sum up the varieties of
Our amorous dalliance. Our viands such
As not alone shall nourish appetite
But strengthen our performance, and when called for,
The choristers of the air shall give us music;
And when we slumber, in a pleasant dream
You shall behold the mountains of vexations
Which you have heaped upon the Roman tyrants
In your free resignation of your kingdom,
And smile at their afflictions.

Antiochus   Hence, you siren!

Courtesan   Are you displeased?

Antiochus   Were all your flatteries
Aimed at this mark? Will not my virtuous anger,
Assisted by contempt and scorn, yield strength
To spurn thee from me? But thou art some whore,
Some common whore, and if thou hast a soul
It hath its being in thy wanton veins,
And will with thy expense of blood become
Like that of sensual beasts.

Metellus   This will not do.

Antiochus   How did my enemies lose themselves to think
A painted prostitute with her charms could conquer
What malice at the height could not subdue?
Is all their stock of malice so consumed
As out of penury they are forced to use
A whore for their last agent?

Courtesan   If thou wert
Ten times a king thou liest. I am a lady,
A gamesome lady of the last edition,
And, though I physic noblemen, no whore.

Metellus   He hath touched her freehold.

Courtesan   Have I lived to have
          My courtesies refused? That I had leave
          To pluck thy eyes out!
          Are you so coy? Thou art a man of snow,
          And thy father got thee in the wane of the moon,
          Dieted with gourd water! O the furies!
          But scorn me not. 'Tis true I was set on
          By the higher powers, but now, for all the wealth
          In Asia, thou shalt not have the favour –
          Though prostrate on the earth thou wouldst implore
                                                    it –
          To kiss my shoestring.

Flaminius   We lose time, my lord.

Courtesan   Foh! How he stinks. I will not wear a rag more
          That he hath breathed on.

                                        Exit Courtesan.

Metellus   Without more ado
          Let him have his sentence.

Flaminius   Drag him hence.

                    Enter Jailer with others.

Antiochus   Are you there? Nay then –

Flaminius   I will not hear him speak. My anger
          Is lost. Why linger you?

Antiochus   Death ends all, however.

                                              Exeunt.

SCENE THREE

Enter Officers, leading in Berecinthius and the First Merchant,
with nooses.

Berecinthius What a skeleton they have made of me. Starve me first
          And hang me after. Is there no conscience extant
          To a man of my order? They have degraded me,

Ta'en away my lions and, to make me roar like 'em,
They have pared the flesh off from my fingers' ends
And then laughed at me. I have been kept in darkness
These five long days, no visitants but devils,
Or men in shapes more horrid, coming at me.
A chafing dish of coals and a butcher's knife
I found set by me, and, inquiring why,
I was told that I had flesh enough of mine own
And if that I were hungry I might freely
Eat mine own carbonadoes and be chronicled
For a cannibal never read of.

Officer   Will you walk, sir?

Berecinthius I shall come too soon, though I creep, to such a
                                                    breakfast.
I ever used to take my portion sitting;
Hanging in the air, 'tis not physical.

Officer   Time flies away, sir.

Berecinthius Why, let him fly, sir. Or, if you please to stay him,
And bind up the bald knave's wings, make use of
                                        my collar –
There is substance in it, I can assure your worship –
And I thank your wisdom that you make distinction
Between me and this starveling. He goes to it
Like a greyhound for killing of sheep in a twopenny
                                                    slip.
But here's a cable will weigh up an anchor,
And yet, if I may have fair play ere I die,
Ten to one I shall make it crack.

Officer   What would you have, sir?

Berecinthius My ballast about me; I shall ne'er sail well else
To the other world. My bark, you see, wants stowage;
But give me half a dozen of hens and a loin of veal
To keep it steady, and you may spare the trouble
Of pulling me by the legs. This drum, well braced,
Defies such foolish courtesies.

1 Merchant   This mirth, good flamen,
Is out of season. Let us think of Elysium,

If we die honest men, or what we there
Shall suffer from the Furies.

Berecinthius   Thou art a fool
To think there are or gods or goddesses.
For the latter, if that she had any power,
Mine – being the mother of 'em – would have
                                                helped me.
They are things we make ourselves. Or, grant there
                                                should be
A hell or an Elysium, sing I cannot
To Orpheus' harp in the one, nor dance in the other.
But if there be a Cerberus, if I serve not
To make three sops for his three heads, that may serve
For something more than an ordinary breakfast,
The cur is devilish hungry. Would I had
Run away with your fellow merchants. I had then
Provided for my fame. Yet, as I am,
I have one request to make, and that, my friends,
Concerns my body, which I pray you grant,
And then I shall die in peace.

Officer   What is it?

Berecinthius   Marry,
That you would be suitors to the proconsul for me
That no covetous Roman, after I am dead,
May beg to have my skin flayed off, or stuff it
With straw like an alligator, and then show it
In fairs and markets for a monster, though
I know the sight will draw more fools to gape on't
Than a camel or an elephant. Aforehand
I tell you: if you do, my ghost shall haunt you.

Officer   You shall have burial, fear not.

Berecinthius   And room enough
To tumble in, I pray you, though I take up
More grave than Alexander. I have ill luck
If I stink not as much as he, and yield the worms
As large a supper.

1 Merchant	Are you not mad to talk thus?

Berecinthius I came crying into the world, and am resolved
　　　　　　To go out merrily: therefore despatch me.

Exeunt.

SCENE FOUR

Enter Metellus and Flaminius.

Metellus There was never such a constancy.

Flaminius 　　　　　　　　　　　　　　You give it
　　　　　　Too fair a name; 'tis foolish obstinacy,
　　　　　　For which he shall without my pity suffer.
　　　　　　What we do for the service of the republic
　　　　　　And propagation of Rome's glorious empire
　　　　　　Needs no defence, and we shall wrong our judgements
　　　　　　To feel compunction for it. Have you given order,
　　　　　　According to the sentence, that the impostor,
　　　　　　Riding upon an ass, his face turned to
　　　　　　The hinder part, may in derision be
　　　　　　Brought through Calipolis?

Metellus 　　　　　　　　　　　　　　Yes; and a paper
　　　　　　Upon his head, in which, with capital letters
　　　　　　His faults inscribed, and by three trumpeters
　　　　　　Proclaimed before him; and that done, to have him
　　　　　　Committed to the galleys. Here comes Sempronius,
　　　　　　To whom I gave the charge.

Enter Sempronius.

Sempronius 　　　　　　　　　　　　I have performed it
　　　　　　In every circumstance.

Flaminius 　　　　　　　　　　How do the people
　　　　　　Receive it?

Sempronius 　　　　　　As an act of cruelty
　　　　　　And not of justice. It drew tears from all
　　　　　　The sad spectators. His demeanour was

In the whole progress worth the observation,
But one thing most remarkable.

Metellus   What was that?

Sempronius When the city-clerk, with a loud voice, read the cause
For which he was condemned – in taking on him
The name of a king – with a settled countenance
The miserable man replied, 'I am so.'
But when he touched his being a cheating Jew,
His patience moved, with a face full of anger
He boldly said, ''Tis false!' I never saw
Such magnanimity.

Flaminius   Frontless impudence rather.

Sempronius Or any thing else you please.

Flaminius   Have you forced on him
The habit of a slave?

Sempronius   Yes, and in that,
Pardon my weakness, still there does appear
A kind of majesty in him.

Flaminius   You look on it
With the eyes of foolish pity that deceives you.

Sempronius This way he comes, and I believe when you see him
You'll be of my opinion.

Officer   (*Within*)   Make way there.

*Enter Officers, leading in Antiochus, his head shaved,
and in the habit of a slave.*

Antiochus Fate, 'tis thy will it should be thus, and I
With patience obey it. Was there ever,
In all precedent maps of misery,
Calamity so drawn out to the life
As she appears in me? In all the changes
Of fortune, such a metamorphosis
Antiquity cannot show us. Men may read there
Of kings deposed and some in triumph led
By the proud insulting Roman, yet they were
Acknowledged such, and died so. Does it not suffice

That the locks of this once royal head are shaved off;
My glorious robes changed to this slavish habit;
This hand that grasped a sceptre manacled;
Or that I have been, as a spectacle,
Exposed to public scorn, if, to make perfect
The cruel reckoning, I am not compelled
To live beyond this, and, with stripes, be forced
To stretch my shrunk-up sinews at an oar,
In the company of thieves and murderers,
My innocence and their guilt no way distinguished,
But equal in our sufferings?

Metellus   You may yet
Redeem all and be happy.

Flaminius   But, persisting
In this imposture, think but what it is
To live in hell on earth, and rest assured
It is your fatal portion.

Antiochus   Do what you please.
I am in your power, but still Antiochus,
King of the Lower Asia – no impostor –
That two and twenty years since lost a battle,
And challenge now mine own, which tyrannous Rome
With violence keeps from me.

Flaminius   Stop his mouth!

Antiochus   This is the very truth; and if I live
Thrice Nestor's years in torture, I will speak
No other language.

Metellus   I begin to melt.

Flaminius   To the galley with him.

Antiochus   Every place shall be
A temple in my penitence to me.

                                        Exeunt.

ACT FIVE

SCENE ONE

Enter Marcellus, proconsul of Sicily, with a letter,
Second Merchant and Third Merchant.

Marcellus	Upon your recantation this galley slave
	Was not Antiochus, you had your pardons
	Signed by the Senate?

2 Merchant   Yes, my lord.

Marcellus   Troth, tell me,
And freely – I am no informer – did you
Believe and know him such, or raised that rumour
For private ends of your own?

3 Merchant   May it please your excellence
To understand the fear of death wrought on us,
In a kind, to turn apostate; besides,
Having proved our testimonies could not help him,
We studied our safeties.

2 Merchant   A desire, too,
For the recovery of goods plundered
From us in Asia by merchants of Carthage,
Urged us to seek redress.

3 Merchant   Our wares kept from us
With strong hand by Flaminius.

Marcellus   In worldly wisdom
You are excusable, but –

3 Merchant   We beseech your honour
Press us no further.

Marcellus   I do not purpose it.
(*Holding up a letter*) Do you know what this contains?

2 Merchant   No, my good lord.

3 Merchant   Perhaps we bear the warrant for our deaths,
As 'tis said of Bellerophon, yet we durst not
Presume to open it.

Marcellus   'Twas manners in you;
But I'll discharge you of that fear. [The Senate
Intends no hurt.   *Opens the letter.*
But your fears are not without foundation;
This letter bears an order for your deaths.
Flaminius pronounces that you remain
A threat to Rome; it seems he fears you will recant
Your recantation. You are to be hanged.
But I will not contradict the Senate's order –
Your lives are safe.

3 Merchant   We thank your lordship.
(*To other Merchant*) He would kill us.

2 Merchant   Without sanction, the worm.

3 Merchant   The viper.]

Marcellus   How is the service of Flaminius spoke of
In Rome?

2 Merchant   With admiration, and many
Divine great honours to him.

Marcellus   The people's voice
Is not oraculous ever. Are you sure
The galley in which your supposed king is chained
Was bound for Syracuse?

3 Merchant   She is now
In the port, my lord.

Marcellus   Titus Flaminius in her?

3 Merchant   Upon my certain knowledge.

Marcellus   Keep yourselves
Concealed till you are called for. When least hoped for,
You shall have justice.

2 Merchant   Your honour's vassals ever.

                                        Exeunt Merchants.

Marcellus	Here, here, it is apparent that the poet
	Wrote truth – though no proof else could be alleged
	To make it good – that though the heavens lay open
	To human wishes, and the Fates were bound
	To sign what we desire, such clouds of error
	Involve our reason, we still beg a curse
	And not a blessing. How many, born unto
	Ample possessions, and like petty kings
	Disposing of their vassals, sated with
	The peace and quiet of a country life,
	Carried headlong with ambition, contend
	To wear the golden fetters of employment,
	Presuming there's no happiness but in
	The service of the state? But when they have tried,
	By a sad experience, the burden of 'em,
	When 'tis not in their power, at any rate
	They would redeem their calm security,
	Mortgaged in wantonness. Alas, what are we
	That govern provinces but preys exposed
	To every subtle spy? And when we have,
	Like sponges, sucked in wealth, we are squeezed out
	By the rough hand of the law, and, failing in
	One syllable of our commission, with
	The loss of what we got with toil, we draw
	What was our own in question.

Enter Cornelia.

You come timely,
To turn my tired thoughts from a sad discourse
That I had with myself.

Cornelia	I rather fear, sir,
	I bring an argument along with me
	That will increase, not lessen, such conceptions
	As I found with you.

Marcellus	Why, sweet, what's the matter?

Cornelia	When I but name Antiochus – though I spare
	To make a brief relation how he died,
	Or what he is, if he now live – a sigh,

And seconded with a tear, I know must fall
As a due tribute to him.

Marcellus   Which I pay
Without compulsion. But why do you
Lance this old sore?

Cornelia   Th'occasion commands it,
And now I would forget it I am forced
In thankfulness to call to memory
The favours for which we must ever owe him.
You had the honour in his court at Sardis
To be styled his friend, an honour Rome and Carthage
Were rivals for, and did deserve the envy
Of his prime minions and favourites.
His magnificent gifts to you
Confirmed his true affection, which you were
More weary to receive than he to give;
Yet still he studied new ones.

Marcellus   Pray you, no more.

Cornelia   O, 'tis a theme, sir, I could ever dwell on;
But since it does offend you, I will speak
Of what concerns myself. He did not blush,
In the height of his felicity, to confess
Fabritius, my lord and father, for
His much-loved kinsman, and as such observed him.
You may please to remember, too, with
What respect and grace he did receive me.
And, at a solemn tilting, when he had
Put on the richest armour of the world,
Smiling, he said – his words are still, and shall be
Writ in the tablet of my heart – 'Fair cousin,'
So he began (and then you thought me fair too),
'Since I am turned soldier, 'twere a solecism
In the language of the war to have no mistress.
And therefore, as a prosperous omen to
My undertakings, I desire to fight,
So you with willingness give suffrage to it,
Under your gracious colours.' And then, loosening
A scarf tied to mine arm, he did entreat me

To fasten it on his. O, with what joy
I did obey him, rapt beyond myself
In my imagination to have
So great a king my servant.

Marcellus   You had too
Some private conference.

Cornelia   And you gave way to it
Without a sign of jealousy, and dispensed with
The Roman gravity.

Marcellus   Would I could again
Grant you like opportunity.
Is this remembered now?

Cornelia   It does prepare
A suit I have – which you must not deny me –
To see the man who, as it is reported,
In the exterior parts nature hath drawn
As his perfect copy. There must be something in him
Remarkable in his resemblance only
Of King Antiochus' features.

Marcellus   'Twas my purpose.
And so much, my Cornelia, Flaminius
Shall not deny us.

Enter Flaminius and Demetrius.

Flaminius   As my duty binds me,
My stay here being but short, I come unsent for
To kiss your lordship's hands.

Marcellus   I answer you
In your own language, sir.
(*Aside*)   And yet your stay here
May be longer than you think.

Flaminius   Most honoured madam,
I cannot stoop too low in tendering of
My humblest service.

Cornelia   You disgrace your courtesy
In overacting it, my lord; I look not
For such observance.

Flaminius   I am most unhappy
If that your excellence make any scruple
Of doubt you may command me.

Cornelia   This assurance
Gives me encouragement to entreat a favour,
In which my lord being a suitor with me,
I hope shall find a grant.

Flaminius   Though all that's mine
Be comprehended in't.

Marcellus   Your promise, sir,
Shall not so far engage you. In respect
Of some familiar passages between
The King Antiochus, when he lived, and us,
And though it needs it not for farther proof
That this is an impostor, we desire
Some conference with him.

Flaminius   For your satisfaction
I will dispense a little with the strictness
Of my commission.
(*To Demetrius*)   Sirrah, tell the captain
To bring him to the proconsul.

Cornelia   His chains took off;
That I entreat too, since I would not look on
The image of a king I so much honoured
Bound like a slave.

Flaminius   See this great lady's will
Be punctually obeyed.

                                        Exit Demetrius.

Marcellus   Your wisdom, sir,
Hath done the state a memorable service
In strangling in the birth this dreadful monster.
And though with some your cruel usage of him
(For so they call your fit severity)
May find a harsh interpretation, wise men
In judgement must applaud it.

Flaminius   Such as are

> Selected instruments for deep designs,
> As things unworthy of 'em, must not feel
> Or passions or affections. And though I know
> The ocean of your apprehensions needs not
> The rivulet of my poor cautions, yet,
> Bold from my long experience, I presume,
> As a symbol of my zeal and service to you,
> To leave this counsel: when you are, my lord,
> Graced or distasted by the state, remember
> Your faculties are the state's, and not your own;
> And therefore have a care the empty sounds
> Of friend or enemy sway you not beyond
> The limits are assigned you. We with ease
> Swim down the stream, but to oppose the torrent
> Is dangerous, and, to go more or less
> Than we are warranted, fatal.

Marcellus   With my thanks
> For your so grave advice, I'll put in practice
> On all occasions what you deliver,
> And study 'em as aphorisms. When the impostor
> Arrives, let us have notice. Pray you walk, sir.

Exeunt.

SCENE TWO

Enter Antiochus, a Captain and Soldiers.

Captain   Wait at the palace gate. There is no fear now
> Of his escape. I'll be myself his guardian
> Till you hear further from me.

Exeunt Soldiers.

Antiochus   What new engine
> Hath cruelty found out to raise against
> This poor demolished rampart? It is levelled
> With the earth already. If there be
> A vial of affliction not poured out yet
> Upon this sinful head, I am prepared,

And will look on the cloud before it break,
Without astonishment. Scorn me not, captain,
As a vain braggart; I will make this good,
And I have strengths to do it. I am armed
With such varieties of defensive weapons,
Lent to me from my passive fortitude,
That there's no torment of a shape so horrid
Can shake my constancy. Where lies the scene now?
Though the hanging of the stage were congealed gore,
The chorus flinty executioners,
And the spectators, if it could be, more
Inhuman than Flaminius, the cue given,
The principal actor's ready.

Captain   If I durst,
I could show my compassion.

Antiochus   Take heed, captain:
Pity in Roman officers is a crime
To be punished more than murder in cold blood.
Bear up. To tell me where I am, I take it,
Is no offence.

Captain   You are in Syracuse,
In the court of Marcellus.

Antiochus   Ha! He was
My creature! And, in my prosperity, proud
To hold dependence of me, though I graced him
With the title of a friend, and his fair lady
In courtship styled my mistress. Can they be
Infected with such barbarism as to make me
A spectacle for their sport?

Enter Marcellus, Flaminius, Cornelia and Servants.

Captain   They are here, and soon
They will resolve you.

Marcellus   (*To Cornelia*)   Be reserved, and let not
The mere resemblance of his shape transport you
Beyond yourself, though I confess the object
Does much amaze me.

Cornelia   You impose, my lord,
What I want power to bear.

Marcellus   Let my example –
Though your fierce passions make war against it –
Strengthen your reason.

Antiochus   Have you taken yet
A full view of me? In what part do I
Appear a monster?

Cornelia   His own voice!

Marcellus   Forbear.

Antiochus Though I were an impostor, as this fellow
Labours you to believe, you break the laws
Of fair humanity in adding to
Affliction at the height; and I must tell you,
The reverence you should pay unto the shape
Of King Antiochus may challenge pity
As a due debt, not scorn. Wise men preserve
Dumb pictures of their friends and look upon 'em
With feeling and affection, yet not hold it
A foolish superstition. But there is
In thankfulness a greater tie on you
To show compassion.

Marcellus   Were it possible
Thou couldst be King Antiochus –

Antiochus   What then?

Marcellus I should both say and do –

Antiochus   Nothing for me
Not suiting with the quality and condition
Of one that owes his loyalty to Rome.
And since it is by the inscrutable will
Of fate determined that the royalties
Of Asia must be conferred upon her –
For what offence I know not – 'tis in vain
For men to oppose it. You express, my lord,
A kind of sorrow for me, in which, madam,
You seem to be a sharer. That you may

Have some proof to defend it, for your mirth's sake
I'll play the juggler, or more subtle gypsy,
And to your admiration reveal
Strange mysteries to you, which, as you are Romans,
You must receive for cunning tricks, but give
No farther credit to 'em.

Flaminius   At your peril
You may give him hearing, but to have faith in him
Neighbours on treason. Such an impudent slave
Was never read of.

Marcellus   I dare stand his charms
With open ears. Speak on.

Antiochus   If so, have at you.
Can you call to your memory when you were
At Sardis with Antiochus, before
His Grecian expedition, what he
With his own hands presented you as a favour,
No third man by to witness it?

Marcellus   Give me leave
To recollect myself. Yes – sure 'twas so –
He gave me a fair sword.

Antiochus   'Tis true, and you
Vowed never to part from it. Is it still
In your possession?

Marcellus   The same sword I have,
And while I live will keep.

Antiochus   Will you not say,
It being two and twenty years since you
Were master of that gift, if now I know it
Among a thousand others, that I have
The art of memory?

Marcellus   I shall receive it
As no common trick. – Fetch all the swords
For mine own use in my armory.
(*Aside to Servant*)   And do you hear –
Do as I give directions.   *Whispers.*

Servant	With all care, sir.

Exit Servant.

Antiochus   And to entertain the time until your servant
Returns, there is no syllable that passed
Between you and Antiochus which I could not
Articulately deliver. You must still
Be confident that I am an impostor,
Or else the trick is nothing.

Enter Servant, with many swords.

Cornelia   Can this be?

Antiochus   O welcome, friend. Most choice and curious swords,
But mine is not among 'em.

Marcellus   Bring in the rest.

Enter another Servant, with more swords.

Antiochus   Ay, this is it.

Marcellus   I know not,
But I am thunderstruck.

Cornelia   I can contain
Myself no longer.

Antiochus   Stay, dear madam. Though
Credulity be excusable in your sex,
To take away all colour of guilt in you,
You shall have stronger proofs. The scarf you gave me,
As a testimony you adopted me
Into your service, I wore on mine armour
When I fought with Marcus Scaurus. And mine eye
Hath on the sudden found a precious jewel
You deigned to receive from me,
Which you wear on your breast.

Cornelia   I acknowledge it was the King Antiochus' gift.

Antiochus   I will
Make a discovery of a secret in it,
Of which you yet are ignorant. Pray you trust it,

For King Antiochus' sake, into my hands.
I thank your readiness. Nay, dry your eyes;
You hinder else the faculty of seeing
The cunning of the lapidary. I can
Pull out the stone, and under it you shall find
My name, and cipher I then used, engraven.

Cornelia   'Tis most apparent. Though I lose my life for't,
These knees shall pay their duty.

Antiochus   By no means.
For your own sake be still incredulous,
Since your faith cannot save me.

Flaminius   'Tis not safe, my lord,
To suffer this.

Marcellus   I am turned statue, or
All this is but a vision.

Antiochus   Your ear, madam,
Since what I now shall say is such a secret
As is known only to yourself and me,
And must exclude a third, though your own lord,
From being of the counsel. Having gained
Access and privacy with you, my hot blood
(No friend to modest purposes) prompted me
With pills of poisoned language, candied o'er
With hopes of future greatness, to attempt
The ruin of your honour. I enforced then
My power to justify the ill, and pressed you
With mountainous promises of love and service.
But when the building of your faith and virtue
Began to totter, and a kind of grant
Was offered, my then sleeping temperance
Began to rouse itself; and breaking through
The obstacles of lust, when most assured
To enjoy a pleasant hour, I let my suit fall,
And with a gentle reprehension taxed
Your forward proneness, but with many vows
Ne'er to discover it, which heaven can witness
I have and will keep faithfully.

Cornelia   This is
The King Antiochus, as sure as I am
The daughter of my mother.

Marcellus   Be advised.

Flaminius   This is little less than treason.

Cornelia   They are traitors,
Traitors to innocence and oppressed justice,
That dare affirm the contrary. The Senate
Must restore him unto his own;
I will die else.

Marcellus   Pray you temper
The violence of your passion.

Antiochus   Live long, madam,
To nobler and more profitable uses.
I am a falling structure, and desire not that
Your honours should be buried in my ruins.
Let it suffice, my lord, you must not see
The sun if, in the policy of state,
It is forbidden. With compassion
Of what a miserable king hath suffered,
Preserve me in your memory.

Flaminius   You stand as
This sorcerer had bewitched you.
(*To the Soldiers*)   Drag him to
His oar, and let his weighty chains be doubled.

Marcellus   For my sake let the poor man have what favour
You can afford him.

Flaminius   Sir, you must excuse me.
(*To Antiochus*) You have abused the liberty I gave you.
But, villain, you pay dear for't. I will trust
The execution of his punishment
To no man but myself; his cries and groans
Shall be my hourly music. So, my lord,
I take my leave abruptly.

Cornelia   May all plagues
That ever followed tyranny pursue thee.

Marcellus   Pray you stay a little.

Flaminius   On no terms.

Marcellus   Yield so much
To my entreaties.

Flaminius   Not a minute, for
Your government.

Marcellus   I will not purchase, sir,
Your company at such a rate. And yet
Must take the boldness upon me to tell you
You must and shall stay.

Flaminius   How!

Marcellus   Nay, what is more,
As a prisoner, not a guest. Look not so high;
I'll humble your proud thoughts.

Flaminius   You dare not do this
Without authority.

Marcellus   You shall find I have
Sufficient warrant, with detaining you,
To take this man into my custody.
(*To Antiochus*)
Though 'tis not in my power – whate'er you are –
To do you further favour, I thus free you
Out of this devil's paws.

Antiochus   I take it as
A lessening of my torments.

Flaminius   You shall answer
This in another place.

Marcellus   But you shall here
Yield an account without appeal for what
You have already done.
(*Hands him the letter*)   You may peruse the letter.
Shake you already? [Your office to Rome
Has been steadfast and unswerving, ever;
Your duties executed with a sweeping
Rigour much admired. But it would appear

Your commission has freed itself of bounds,
Assumed imperious command, and at once
Your judgement and wisdom falter. You have not
The authority to contrive your sinecure
To allow such gross deceit of Rome's interest.
I recognise your wish to deny Antiochus
His name, but your stratagems, your corrupt means
Of disavowal, far exceed your remit.
Sir, it is not of your administration
To extort false testimony under fear of death.
Fear distorts a man, as I see you quiver now,
And he becomes willing to relinquish himself
Of any nervous untruths that might spare him.
'Tis a crime against Rome to pronounce such lies,
'Tis a greater crime to bleed this blasphemy
From innocents. Did not you intend a warrant
For the lives of these two merchants?
The Senate elects to pardon these men;
Yet your letter countermands this ruling,
It pretends danger they do not present.]
You took bribes of the Carthaginian merchants,
To detain their lawful prize, and for your
Sordid ends abused the trust committed
By the state to right its vassals. [You go unchecked;
You know not where your power ends. This
                       governance
Is indiscreet, reckless;] the wise Senate,
As they will reward your good and faithful service,
Cannot, in justice, without punishment
Pass o'er your ill. Guiltiness makes you dumb;
But till that I have leisure, and you find
Your tongue, to prison with him.

Flaminius   I prove too late –
As heaven is merciful, man's cruelty
Never escapes unpunished.

                    Exeunt Soldiers with Flaminius.

Antiochus   How a smile
Labours to break forth from me. But what is
Rome's pleasure shall be done with me?

Marcellus   Pray you think, sir,
A Roman, not your constant friend, that tells you
You are confined unto an island prison
With a strong guard upon you.

Antiochus   Then 'tis easy
To prophesy I have not long to live,
Though the manner how I shall die is uncertain.
(*To Cornelia*) Nay, weep not. Since 'tis not in you to
                                                    help me,
These showers of tears are fruitless. May my story
Teach potentates humility, and instruct
Proud monarchs, though they govern human things,
A greater power does raise, or pull down, kings.

                                    Flourish. Exeunt.

FINIS

A Nick Hern Book

This edition of *Believe What You Will*
first published in Great Britain in 2005
as a paperback original by
Nick Hern Books Limited
14 Larden Road, London W3 7ST
in association with the
Royal Shakespeare Company

Cover design by Andy Williams, RSC Graphics

Typeset by Country Setting, Kingsdown, Kent CT14 8ES
Printed and bound in Great Britain
by Bookmarque, Croydon, Surrey

A CIP catalogue record for this book is available from
the British Library

ISBN-13   978 1 85459 861 5
ISBN-10   1 85459 861 9